Johnny Sexton

Book

A Life of Passion and Perseverance in Rugby

Bob
— Thought You
Would Like This
Stan!

Nicholas Hoffman

Chapter 1

My first sporting arena was the soccer pitch at Kildare Place Primary School. It's a ten-minute walk from where I now reside, a collection of pebble-dashed buildings with a small patch of grass in between.

That pitch was the first place I ever kicked a ball in fury. There is genuine rage.

The keepy-uppies didn't worry me. I practised them for hours on my own in our small back garden in Rathgar, a busy area south of Dublin that is also near to where I currently live.

Dad issued the challenge: twenty quid if I could reach 200, which he quickly changed to 300. He'd sit in the kitchen, with his recliner slanted so that he could keep one eye on his newspaper and one on me. When the ball touched the grass, I'd check to see if he was watching.

I never figured him out.

I went to bed the night before in the jersey, ball beside my bed, and didn't sleep a wink. Winners were announced on television.

We were told after the exercises that we will contact you if we made it. I waited impatiently. I eventually stopped pestering my parents to see if anything had arrived in the mail, and I stopped asking Mr Morton, who served as both principal and PE instructor.

Mr Morton was the teacher who advised me I needed to go into goal that time. I was furious. We were leading Taney Primary School 1-0 at the break, due to a stunning goal from our number ten, me.

Years later, Kildare Place returned the letter to me. They still kept it on file, and someone felt it would be humorous for me to reflect on.

According to what I've heard, Jerry Sexton - Dad - was a large, strong scrum-half talented enough to be selected in the first ever Ireland Schools team in 1975, with a handful of potential internationals, notably Moss Finn, who played in Ireland's 1982 Triple Crown-winning squad.

Dad was also an international, as far as I was concerned. He'd represented his country. I had seen a photo of him wearing a green jersey with a shamrock on the crest and shoulder-length hair.

I used to enjoy hearing stories about Dad. Syl Delahunt, an old acquaintance from UCD, told me that several Dublin clubs wanted Dad to join them after graduation. Club alickadoos used to mistake Syl for Dad - they looked so like - and serve him pints.

Finally, Dad chose Bective Rangers in Donnybrook. He never completely fulfilled his promise, owing to injuries, but he remained connected in Bective, primarily as a coach.

That's probably not everything I acquired from Grandad John. Older Milltown members recall him as a stickler for golfing detail, whether it was related to the rulebook or technique. He was quick to contact a journalist if something was misreported. Dermot Gilleece, a golf writer, once referred to his harsh style. Since then, whenever Grandad John left a message, he signed off as 'Mr Gruff'.

Jody Fanagan, the Walker Cup golfer who broke my grandfather's course record, told Gilleece a story about him. He once asked Jody what he saw when he stood on the tee. Jody said he looked both sides of the fairway.

He died when I was fourteen. The post-funeral reception was held at Milltown, where I was a junior member. I remember slipping out for nine holes while the adults were at a reception at the bar, but my heart wasn't into it. It did not feel right.

In my memories of him, health was always a concern. Emphysema ultimately claimed his life. He drank and smoked heavily. When we saw him in the hospital in his final days, he was wired up to a variety of tubes, and his chest was dark from the poison in his lungs. I recall the terrible rattle in his chest.

Dad advised me, "That's why you should never smoke."

Mum presumably smoked to cope with the stress of being a working mother. Gillian's mother, a hairdresser, started Rathgar Hair Studio, located in the heart of Rathgar hamlet, just a few weeks after her birth.

They say you should never do business with friends or family, yet Mum and Dad did exactly that, purchasing the premises' lease with a buddy. Dad is an accountant, so he prepared the business plan. My parents sat at the kitchen table on a Friday night, browsing through books while their children ravaged around them.

It was only as I got older that I realized how hard they worked and how stressed they were. Mum worked six days a week, including late Thursdays and Friday. On those days, Dad would arrive home before her and cook dinner for us, except for Thursdays, when he would also arrive late and our childminder would make dinner.

He had a difficult routine, too. For several years, he worked for a lumber company at Artane, on Dublin's northside, which required him to leave early to avoid cross-town traffic.

I was a rather serious kid who wasn't particularly good at mixing. Uncle Willie often nicknamed me a "worry wart." I was shy in unfamiliar surroundings.

I felt confident on the soccer surface at Kildare Place and in Bective, where I played mini-rugby. But if Dad took me to Bushy Park Rangers for a tryout, I'd be quiet and reserved.

According to child psychologists, the eldest child is often

competitive, seeking parental approval. Only on rare occasions did I get into significant trouble, and when I did, I was consumed by guilt and couldn't sleep for days.

The following morning, I was sent down to the Late Shopper with my pocket money to confess my wrongdoing. The merchant accepted the money but appeared amused by the entire situation.

Dad has mellowed with age, but he used to have a short fuse and would not put up with anything we said. You'd get a hug at bedtime, but if you did something wrong or didn't give it your all, he'd get upset.

I have no problem with Dad giving me the odd clip. I probably deserved it, and I don't believe it did me any harm.

He was a product of the harsh boarding school environment. His parents were both busy in Listowel, so attending boarding school made sense. His anecdotes about corporal punishment at Castleknock captivated us. Whenever he started a statement with 'When I was in boarding school …', our ears perked up.

He told us fantastic stories of a priest known as the Boxer, so named for obvious reasons. According to Dad, the Boxer would greet you on the corridor with a smile and a 'Good morning', but if your shirt was unkempt or your tie was undone, he'd abruptly snap: 'Your tie is undone, kid!' Then he would deliver a lifeless arm. Any misbehaviour resulted in a cane across the palm, not once, but multiple times. Hearing about such an event excited us.

It's no surprise Dad came out of there with a hardened mentality. The irony is that I find it difficult to discipline my own children, Luca, Amy, and Sophie. Laura warns me not to let them get away with things so easy, but they've had me wrapped around their little fingers. With them, I'm a total softie.

She took off her slipper and went to spank Mark on the arse.

He swung his hips, Mum took a 'fresh air', and we all tumbled about laughing. Then she lost it completely. She hurled the slipper, a big piece of footwear with a strong heel, at us. Jerry and I both ducked, and Mark got it on the temple. He bawled. Mum was also in tears, especially as Mark's eye began to swell and blacken. We still tease her about it every now and then.

Mark and I are quite close. He turned out to be an excellent rugby player, a strong, intelligent centre who won the All-Ireland League with St Mary's. He was talented enough to make it as a professional but was forced to retire due to an injury. He is now a coach, having led Ireland's Under-20s win consecutive Grand Slams. He's someone I frequently consult for his thoughts on the game.

It was different when we were children. We fought all the time. Naturally, I felt protective of him in school. I recall sitting with him in Junior Infants during his awful first day, sobbing uncontrollably. Overall, he was a satisfactory company when it fit my needs, but if I had a better option, I would choose it. It may get niggly when we are all indoors in the evening.

There were six of us sharing a three-bedroom house. When I was in my mid-teens, and the parents could afford it, they converted the attic and moved me up there. However, before then, nighttime was never a peaceful, relaxing event. Gillian, as the only girl, had her own room, while the lads shared a room: myself and Mark on bunk beds, Jerry to one side. The entire structure resembled a raft. If one of us moved, the entire structure creaked. Then the debates and scrapping would begin.

Mum tells me that as a two-year-old, I regularly tried everything I could to keep dad from leaving the house. As soon as he got home from work, I'd steal his keys and conceal them somewhere, or I'd sneak one of his shoes behind the sofa.

This was never going to work as a long-term strategy, however. If I wanted to spend more time with Dad, I would need to accompany him to Bective. And that is what happened.

Mum was fed up with looking after four children on Tuesdays, Thursdays, Saturdays and Sundays. She insisted on Dad taking at least one of us with him. Usually, this was me. I was not whining.

This is where I first played rugby. I still have trophies from Under-7 blitzes, as well as a photo from when we won an Under-10 tournament, in which we were wearing club jerseys borrowed from a team several years our older - they were so long on us that they leaked out the bottom of our shorts. We were the club's inaugural minis section, founded by the late Joe Nolan, the club president at the time and a wonderful man.

Every Sunday morning, we trained or played games on a strip of grass outside the clubhouse, which is now covered by a parking lot and terracing. Before kick-off, one of the dads cleared the surface of beer bottles and cigarette packs, and any other incriminating evidence left over from the night before.

I enjoyed that element of Bective, that we were from various backgrounds yet remained close. I believe it was beneficial for me to have that experience before pursuing a privileged, fee-paying education at St Mary's College.

Between September and April, I'd be at Bective's training pitches in Glenamuck, pestering Johnny O'Hagan for a ball - Hago was the Bective bagman and a good friend of Dad's. Dad and I wouldn't come home until about 9.30 or 10 p.m., when my siblings were asleep.

By then, I'd have found my own game, most likely a two-a-side match with Mark and the O'Flanagan brothers, Stuart and Barry. Tim, their father, was both the club doctor and our family's general practitioner. He and his wife Carol were close friends with my parents. Stuart is now one of the doctors in Leinster and Ireland.

Donnybrook was a big, infrequently crowded playground on Sundays. Even if there were games on the front and back pitches, there was plenty of mischief to be had on the tennis courts, behind the main stand, and behind the clubhouses at each end. If it rained, we could play rugby in the Bective hall until a light bulb shattered and we had to flee for safety.

Later, it was time for Sunday dinner. We'd been eating crisps and peanuts all day and had no appetite. Dad saw this as no excuse. As a boarding-school veteran, he couldn't bear the thought of meals going uneaten.

You will sit here until you have completed all of the food on your plates, he stated. So we sat there for hours at a time, interrupted only by trips to the bathroom to flush the Brussels sprouts we'd snuck out in our pockets.

Bective was only in Division Three, but they were fighting hard for promotion under the leadership of Noel McQuilkin, a gruff Kiwi whose son Kurt played center. Dad was Noel's assistant, which provided me access to all places.

From the age of eight to eleven or twelve, I was a fixture in the Bective dressing room, even when Dad wasn't coaching. I'd just grab a couple of Jaffa Cakes from Hago's cache, sit in the corner, and take in the conversation and fumes from the Deep Heat tubes.

We were someplace up north with a large traveling party, and the celebrations were huge. Dad handed me £20 to grab myself a drink and a bag of peanuts, so I went outside with the other kids.

I lost the chance. When he came seeking it, I tried to lie and say I had already handed it to him. He knew this was false. He lost the rag next to me in front of everyone. It wasn't that I'd lost the money, though I'm sure he was irritated about that, too. He was furious because I had lied to him. I felt humiliated.

The ride home was an unusual experience. The bus was filled with drink and song, and there I was, alone up front, feeling sore, arms crossed, staring out the window.

The Bective players attempted to wind me up by calling my name from the back and ducking their heads when I looked around. Then one of them would give me the two fingers in jest, and I would return them. They called me, determined to make me smile.

I eventually warmed up, but Dad maintained a cold front. I suppose he wanted to teach me a lesson. He had strong beliefs about doing the right thing.

Fortunately, there was one place where I could do no wrong, never got in trouble, and was treated like a king.

Listowel.

Chapter 2

My father's hometown is a gorgeous location in north Kerry, a small town with a great reputation because of its two yearly events, Writers' Week in May and Listowel Races in September.

Its most famous resident is unquestionably John B. Keane, a dramatist and writer. John B. He died in 2002, yet he remains a prominent figure in the community. His tavern, which is currently run by his son Billy, is a popular tourist site.

Granny rented a Sega Mega Drive from the video store across the street for the two weeks I'd be there, which was a wonderful pleasure since we didn't have anything like this at home. I spent hours playing video games. Or my grandfather, Daddy John, as we called him to prevent confusion with Grandad John Nestor, would take me to pitch and putt. Most evenings, Daddy John would take me to a tavern to play pool against the locals. It might have been 10 p.m., past my bedtime at home. However, there were no rules in Listowel.

My first exposure with paid sports was during pool challenge games at Flanagan's or the Saddle Bar. We'd be up against farmers, the type of characters you'd see in John B's plays. Country cute.

We were attractive enough, a real double-act, taking alternate photos. Daddy John was competitive. He would carefully study each shot, whispering strategies into my ear. The winners held the table. No celebrations, only Daddy John's somber wink of acceptance as the next contender racked the balls. Holding the table for a few games made you feel like you owned the area.

We might not get home until after midnight, and if there was golf from the United States on television, we'd stay up and watch it until my eyelids dropped.

I became quite close to Daddy John. I never called him Grandad to prevent confusion with my mother's father. He wouldn't have let it regardless. He was determined not to age.

My father's four brothers would take great joy in teasing me about being a Dub, especially when the football final was on. They would remind me I'm part Kerry. It's probably the fiery half, the naughty side, that gets me in trouble.

Ballybunion was amazing because there was always something happening. We played enormous, highly competitive games of family football on one of the beaches, with field markings scraped out on the rough sand with a stick: usually myself, Mark, Roy, a bunch of uncles, and my Auntie Rachel, Mum's sister, who was a terrific player and the tomboy of the family.

Perhaps there was golf. Mum stipulated that if Dad went golfing, he had to bring one of his boys along. That was the agreement, and there were no disputes. I'd get to caddy for my dad at Ballybunion, where my Uncle John was the club captain, and occasionally, when the course ranger wasn't looking, one of my uncles would throw a ball down for me to hit.

I don't get to Kerry as much as I'd like these days, but I want my children to experience the majesty of the place. Billy Keane, my main point of contact, still operates the family bar when he isn't penning Munster rugby columns for the Irish Independent.

My chances of becoming a decent rugby player improved dramatically when I was transferred to St Mary's College in Rathmines, a twenty-minute walk from Rathgar. Mum claims she gave up cigarettes to help with school tuition, and that the sacrifice was worthwhile. She often says, 'Mary's was the best thing I ever did for my boys'.

Mary's provided me more than rugby. I developed lifelong friends there and had several teachers who had a huge beneficial impact on me.

It boosted my confidence that I could repeat fourth grade, which meant I went from being one of the youngest in my group at Kildare Place to one of the oldest in my class at Mary's Junior School.

However, it took me some time to settle. There was conflict among new classmates, and I was undoubtedly to blame. I was keen to make an impression, whether it was in PE, the schoolyard, or on the rugby field. It didn't take long until people's noses were out of joint.

At 10 years old, I was still a scrap of a thing, a scrum-half like my father, but a confident, combative one who refused to give an inch. This was partly due to something I overheard my father say to his friends at the pub in Bective.

It was not part of an intentional plan. It was only me. Being on edge in a physically tough sport is probably not a bad thing. However, your strongest qualities as a sportsperson might also be your worst characteristics as a person.

I ended up best friends with Eoghan, Colin, and Brian, but things were difficult for a while. They were understandably territorial, and they had a numerical advantage over me, so they immediately pushed me away whenever they could. Mum recalls instances when I would arrive home from school in a nasty mood.

Being good at a team sport usually increases your popularity, but this was not always the case for me. One day during my first year at Mary's, Dave Breslin, our PE teacher who also coached the senior school's Junior Cup (Under-15) squad, singled me out in the sports hall. He brought five or six of the Js in the middle of class and threw me a ball. None of the priests were still teaching lessons, but a small community of Spiritan Fathers lived in a building adjacent to the school. Father Flavin and Father McNulty were passionate about rugby. My guess is that they subscribed to Sky Sports before other

Irish households did.

Father Flavin discussed having a saucer-shaped backline in attack. It offered us twelve-year-olds a clearer picture of how we should position ourselves to run on to the ball. Perhaps the St Mary's coaches saw that we needed to be smart technically and tactically because we didn't have the same numbers as some of our rivals.

Rugby truly took off in February and March, during cup season. That was the first time I felt truly a part of the school, when all rivalries were put aside. Being up for Mary's was all that mattered.

We were not required to attend cup matches. It was simply expected that you would go, wearing your blue rugby jersey with the white star-shaped insignia and singing your heart out.

It helped that the juniors made cup runs to the finals during my first two years at the school. Cup weeks were huge. We'd all be herded together in the schoolyard to practice the different songs and chants. In art class, we'd create posters to promote the match.

Then match day would arrive. There are no afternoon classes. Yessss!

Four or five of us would be picked up by someone's mother and driven to Donnybrook or Lansdowne Road, where the finals were played. Blue face paint, with a school tie wrapped around the head in Samurai style. Then it was through the old turnstiles at the Bective end and straight into the stand, where we'd be crammed tightly together as a block of blue, led by the cheerleaders. We'd be on our feet the entire time, shouting out the songs and becoming utterly hoarse by the end.

We all adored Richie. He offered so much wonderful energy, encouragement, and fun. I still like him a lot and we communicate daily. He was my English teacher for three years, and he is one of those professors who can command respect without being harsh. Richie isn't really stern. He has petite, gentle features, flashing eyes behind enormous spectacles, and a massive, silver walrus moustache.

His son, Eoghan Hughes, was once a rival but has now become a good friend, and he continues to organize Christmas reunions for our group. Because our house was on Hughes' way home from training and matches, Richie would frequently give me a lift. It seemed like we never passed a McDonald's or a gas station without him stopping to get us a Big Mac or a Mars Bar and a can of Coke.

I suppose what made us all so loyal to Richie was his personal dedication to the school, the squad, and doing things correctly. I have a picture of him at one of those cup matches, down at the front of the Donnybrook stand, celebrating a try alongside the rest of us. Teachers were usually present to maintain discipline and keep an eye out for any rowdiness, particularly when the opposing team was attempting attempts at goal. But in my memory, Richie is just crazy about Mary's score, just like the rest of us.

He was a rugby aficionado. In English class, we could always tell when he was willing to be sidetracked by a conversation about the previous day's cup match in Donnybrook. He always had a copy of the Irish Times folded between his books, so we'd ask him to read the match report. We believe that assessing the report's quality has educational value. He never needed much convincing.

It would soon turn into a wide discussion regarding the game. Richie loves to talk.

Winning was vital to him, but it was not the sole consideration. He was inclusive. I'm not sure what the substitution rules were for those Provincial Cup games, but he appeared to have as many players on the bench as on the field, and they all looked great in their school tracksuits. Some of those men had no chance of ever getting it onto the pitch for the A team, but they had trained all season and he wanted them to be engaged on big days, when we might be able to leave class an hour early to have a pre-match bowl of soup in the school cafeteria.

Being part of the A squad was really crucial. I remember how upset Cormac Waldron was when he had to skip a week of training around Christmas because his family was going on vacation. Richie put him at ease.

You must enjoy your vacation, Cormy, he said. Bring me a stick of rock.

My Leinster and Ireland teammates are probably unaware that I used to say those three prayers in the dressing room, just before we huddled up. Or that I used to attend mass on the eve of Test matches in Dublin. I'd leave the Shelbourne Hotel and go down to St Teresa's Church on Clarendon Street. It's not a superstition, and I'm not praying to win the man-of-the-match award. It's simply part of who I am. I believe. I have faith.

Richie occasionally prayed for anything rugby-related. In 2009, I was cited for kicking Munster's Lifeimi Mafi during a Magners League match at Thomond Park. When I told Richie I was in danger of being suspended, he promised to light a few candles in Rathfarnham's church. I received a two-week suspension, but Richie did his best for me. As always.

Mary's U13s winning the Provincial Cup in 1999 had little to do with heavenly inspiration. We had a fantastic staff and were really well prepared.

I was now the team captain and played out of the half. We exercised after school on Tuesdays and Thursdays at Kenilworth Square, a lovely park with three pitches nestled among Victorian red-brick residences. We had matches on Wednesdays or Saturdays, perhaps both, and possibly circuit training on Mondays.

The front pitch would be congested at lunchtime, but Father McNulty planned handling drills in the space between the junior school and the military wall' - St Mary's is close to an army barracks.

Hands facing the passerby, fingers spread, hips square, taking and giving.

He didn't do it alone. Paul Andreucetti, a former Leinster and Ireland player whose son John played for the team, and Father McNulty taught the backs once a week.

When it came to league matches, a number of the seniors would also pitch in, which was a huge assistance. We even had a video analyst, as is customary in any decent coaching setup, so our triumph over Willow Park in the final at Templeville - the home of St Mary's College RFC - was recorded for posterity.

I still have the dvd. The sound and camera quality are both awful, but the rugby is not. It was an excellent game. Willow took the lead right after halftime, against the run of play. I had a misunderstanding with my scrum-half, Brian McDermott, after a scrum closed our line. You can see I was irritated.

We kept playing, and our full-back, Killian Browne, scored a fantastic try that demonstrated the merits of all those lunchtime handling drills behind the military wall. The move featured five or six perfectly timed passes. The try provoked a major pitch invasion by Mary's supporters. We won 8 to 5.

Dad's voice can be heard on the DVD of the Under-13s final during the anxious second half. I'm down on one knee, winded, when he says, 'Get up, Jonathan!'I immediately get back on my feet. It is hilarious.

I'm sure there were numerous occasions when Dad wanted to meddle during sports or training. He was a coach, after all. Only once can I recall him getting irritated from the sidelines. Father Flavin used to lose the rag with us on occasion, and for a priest, he could use some colourful language. One day, Dad simply told him to shut up because he couldn't be talking to us like that. And that was all.

We'd play Manhunt in the woods behind the courts, using our racquets to hit each other with acorns. If Dad wanted us to return home for dinner, he would come to the rear gate and whistle. It only took one whistle for us to stop whatever we were doing.

Mark and I were decent tennis players. In fact, for a while, I was more into tennis than rugby. At the age of thirteen, I was selected for a Leinster panel, which required me to attend training sessions on Tuesday and Thursday evenings.

Mum didn't only drive me around. She observed every detail. Tennis remains her favourite sport. I can still get sucked in by it if I witness a nice match on television. My biggest issue with the sport in my teens was the level of cheating that occurred at age-grade events.

You couldn't always count on an official umpire at lower levels, and parents would frequently serve as line judges in games featuring their own children. Their eyesight appeared to be affected at times by their strong desire to see their children prosper.

It came to the point where it felt like you had to shoot at least a metre inside the line to avoid being called out. There were always questionable calls. It used to drive me crazy.

Mark simply couldn't handle it. At one tournament, he simply smashed his racket off the court, yelled abuse at the offending mother, and stormed out. I'd be able to maintain a lid on things for the most part, but there's only so much you can handle.

The final straw for me came at a tournament at Naas, also known as the fifth major. I made it to the boys' under-13 final. Mum and Dad came along for this one. And I was killing it. I won the first set six games to love and was far up in the second set when my opponent, whom I will not identify, began crying and told the umpire he wanted to take a break.

He left the court for perhaps fifteen or twenty minutes and went to the washroom, where his mother, father, and coach attempted to calm him down. Meanwhile, I was left alone on the court, twiddling my thumbs.

If that toilet stop was a frantic attempt to disrupt my momentum, it was successful. After all that time spent waiting on the court, I lost my rhythm, dropped the following few games, and eventually lost the match. Is it a miraculous comeback or just plain gamesmanship?

I was inconsolable. As runner-up, I received an alarm clock. Cheers. Such experiences put your love of sports to the test.

It turned out to be a difficult task. The only difference between the girls was that one wore a headband. They opted not to change ends to make things less confusing, but I became distracted and lost focus.

Chapter 3

Joan Manning was struggling with fifth-year French. It was probably difficult enough teaching the subjunctive without me interrupting the class. Every time she turned to clarify a verb ending on the whiteboard, I used my foot to turn off the projector. Cue the laughing. Ms Manning gave a long-suffering sigh as she came down to turn the machine back on. Again.

So she advised me to take my sense of humour elsewhere. I was not accepted in her French class. That was it: my first red card. And it wasn't like I could simply switch teachers. There was only one fifth-year class for honors French.

Dad was not pleased when I described the problem. I told him not to worry. I could switch to home economics. It was supposed to be easy. But he was not having any of it.

I was lucky in that if I had any problems at St Mary's, I could report them to Brian Wall. He was the dean of studies for fourth, fifth, and sixth-year boys, a guidance counselor, and an outstanding chemistry and math instructor. I was in his class for both, so I saw him frequently. He managed to find time to teach at the Institute of Education, a kind of upmarket cramming college in town known for offering high-quality notes on each subject. Brian used to sneak me his Institute chemistry notes on the side.

As a child, whenever I was taken to see someone in the hospital, I used to like prowling around the wards. My favorite television show at the time was ER. Later, anytime I got wounded while playing rugby, I would constantly question my physicians about it. I'd look at scans with them and inquire about strategies to speed up the healing process.

What really drew me to medicine was the work experience I had in

Transition Year with an orthopaedic surgeon, Dr David Moore, who was an old school friend of Dad's. Every morning at 6 a.m., David would pick me up from the house and drive me to St James' Hospital, where we would scrub up and go into surgery. I'd get to observe him perform a variety of surgeries. I was fascinated.

To enter into medicine, you needed to have an excellent Leaving Cert, but I thought I could do it. With Laura's assistance, I completed a respectable Junior Cert - three As and seven Bs - which I was very pleased with. I was determined to please my parents.

My father welcomed the idea of me pursuing medicine. He was ambitious for me in rugby, but he wasn't convinced that I should put all my eggs in the pro rugby basket.

It was the early noughties, barely a few years into the professional era. From what he'd heard, only a few players made decent money: Brian O'Driscoll and possibly Keith Wood. And it had a short career. You can't just be a rugby player, Dad explained. You will need something else.

Rugby was a little frustrating that season. I had my heart set on being out-half of a good senior side that featured a dozen players returned from the previous season, the most of whom were now in their last year. These were guys I admired, but I didn't let it show.

The fact that we were drawn against Terenure in the first round, and they had a guy named Conor Gildea starting at 10, made it really difficult for me. Gildea was rumored to be the next big thing; my purported friends were always bragging about how clever he was, simply to wind me up. I was dying to get a crack from him. But, on this occasion, I simply had to put on my tracksuit and suck it up.

At least we demolished them and I made it onto the pitch at the end.

Dave Breslin, who currently coaches the SCT alongside former

Ireland full-back Rodney O'Donnell, brought me on with a minute remaining.

The night before, a storm swept in - I believe meteorologists even named it - and the weather was horrible. On the morning of the game, I felt completely relaxed because it had been announced that it would be postponed. Dad refused to play the game. You couldn't let children out in that.

They did. When we arrived at the stadium, the corner flags were almost horizontal, the temperature was Arctic, and the rain was relentless. But there was no mention of a postponement. Ireland played there a week later, and the pitch would require time to recover. We were moving ahead. By the end of the warm-up, our tracksuits were completely soaked.

The footage can be viewed online. The photo is shaky because the cameraman was straining to keep his camera steady in the wind. You see me jogging, shoulders slightly bowed against the elements, a number 16 shirt blowing.

Was I prepared for this? Not in a formal training setting. But I had seen all the amazing drop-goals on video. Joel Stransky in the 1995 World Cup final, Jerry Guscott for the 1997 Lions, and Michael Kiernan against England in 1985, the year I was born, all played on the same pitch at the same end. I had kicked one for the Under-13s versus St Michael's on Kenilworth's top pitch. I can still picture the ball going between the posts and landing in the old elm trees.

A drop-goal puts less pressure on the team than a penalty because it is scored in open play while on the run. So I was quite calm as the forwards knocked the ball up from a lineout, resulting in a ruck on the 22 in front of the Havelock Square posts. Scrum-half Simon Gibney had to throw the ball back into the wind, forcing me to stoop to grab it about six inches off the sodden turf - not a bad thing in this case because there's less tolerance for error with the 'drop' element of the drop-kick. I made a clean connection, and it sailed straight between the poles and into the empty terrace, not exceptionally high but sufficiently enough. Boom.

Looking back, I'm not sure if I fully appreciated or absorbed anything. There was scarcely a moment to pause and contemplate, from the cup presentation to the crowded dressing room to the official reception back at Mary's, with the entire school cheering us on stage, the venue decked out in blue and white, and everyone's parents and siblings present. It was all a swirl of noise and happiness.

I did not forget Ian O'Herlihy's vow, however. I kept him to his word.

Winning the Schools Cup provided prizes. We were invited to attend an international school tournament in Japan the following month. The principal decided that the squad should be made up of males from fourth and fifth years, as sixth-year students needed to focus on their Leaving Cert preparations. Those unlucky men missed an amazing holiday.

We stayed at a boarding school in Fukuoka. Thirty of us crowded into one cramped, scorching room with triple bunk beds. We were pitted against a massive team from Wesley College in Auckland the initial morning we arrived. Some of those guys wore beards. They really hammered us. We won something called the Consolation Cup.

We were not the only Irish travelers to Japan in 2002. This was the summer in Saipan. The Sexton family, like many others in Ireland, was divided over Roy Keane's dispute with Republic of Ireland manager Mick McCarthy. You couldn't be undecided on this. It was a civil war.

Three years later, however, he was chastised for being selfish and prioritizing himself over the Ireland team. I argued that Keane was correct in standing up for his opinion that an international team to a World Cup should demand the finest possible preparation. I appreciated his courage in standing by his convictions. Dad was having none of it. He may have been a big Manchester United supporter and a big Keane admirer, but he was firmly in McCarthy's side on this one.

It was the summer of my seventeenth birthday. My goal for the upcoming rugby season was to be selected for the Irish Schools team. It would be my last chance, because I would be overage in my last school year, according to the regulations in effect at the time.

The Irish Schools team played all their major matches towards the end of the season, following the cup campaigns. But you really needed to make your impact in October with your regional team. A good interpro series would put you in the 'Probables' category for the crucial final trial around Christmas time. Get on the Probables, and the task is half done. So the theory went, anyway.

I got the first few stages correct. I performed well in the Leinster trials, was chosen for a trip to Leicester and Yorkshire in November, and started in the win over Ulster in Donnybrook. We didn't play particularly well, but I believed I had a reasonable chance of reaching the Probables if I could put on a nice show against Munster.

The training session on the eve of the game was going well until I attempted to execute a switch with a teammate and he accidently stood on my ankle, causing ligament damage. George Byron was from St Michael's. Certain details remain with you.

That took me out of the Munster game. Fergal Lawlor of Roscrea succeeded me. He made the most of his opportunity as Leinster cruised to victory in Cork. I feared the worst.

The first part of that calculation came out alright. We enjoyed a protracted Cup run, defeating Blackrock in an attritional semi-final replay to advance to our second straight final at Lansdowne Road. As luck would have it, our opponents were Terenure's Conor Gildea and his mates.

Laura was strolling beside Bushy Park one day, and some of the Terenure team members were following us, close enough for me to hear their intimidation tactics.

So I was ecstatic when we won their place. It was merely 'friendly', and I wasn't even scheduled to play because it was the morning after a Schools interpro, and I was supposed to rest. I was told I could sit on the bench but not come on. Only in an emergency, I was informed.

Mary fell behind at halftime. That qualified as an emergency.

For some reason, we had to switch pitches at halftime. This is when I recognized my opportunity. I subbed in, and the coaches didn't notice. I was crazy there, getting into fights. When I gave one of them a black eye, he threatened me with revenge: "I have an older brother and he's coming after you, ya prick!"

However, Terenure had the last laugh. The 2003 Cup final could not have been more different than the previous year. For starters, it was played during a heatwave, with temperatures reaching 24 degrees in mid-March. St Patrick's Day fell on a Monday, so it was a long weekend with a holiday vibe, and a large crowd flocked to Lansdowne Road to witness.

The Transition Year student, who had nothing to lose, suddenly felt like he was carrying the weight of the entire world on his shoulders. Almost the entire school was watching us warm up on the back pitch, cheering and chanting.

Former Mary's students streamed out of the Lansdowne clubhouse bars, with beer on their breath. They all formed a sort of tunnel as we returned under the east stand to the main pitch. I could see guys from the previous year's team yelling encouragement.The exit is on the left. I was reminded of the game-winning penalty I took from a similar angle to defeat Rob Kearney's Clongowes squad in the first round.

I was not even selected on the bench. Perhaps they felt they couldn't justify having two Leinster 10s in the squad, so they went with the Munster out-half. I was wondering what would happen if they got pummeled by France first. But no. They won all three games. I tortured myself by going up to see them defeat England at Templeville Road.

Another successful Cup campaign would undoubtedly be beneficial. We entered as joint favourites with Blackrock. There was only one problem: we had been drawn against each other in the first round.

I was wired for the game. Completely wired. I was captain that season, my third season on the senior panel, my final year at St Mary's, and only a few months away from turning nineteen. I was a tough captain, too.

We were all best pals by halftime versus Blackrock, though. We led 17-3 and were on track for our third consecutive Senior Cup triumph over 'Rock, no small feat. I, too, felt completely in charge. I was striking the ball well, converting two tries and missing one goal. The Irish Times described me as 'the most accomplished player on the field'.

Unfortunately, the report also referred to the game as 'one of the greatest cup comebacks'. I remember it better than any other Schools Cup match I've played, partly because it was my last, and partly because Leo Cullen, who was coaching the 'Rock side, and Luke Fitzgerald, a sprightly sixteen-year-old who came off their bench after the break and made a difference, reminded me of it frequently over the years.

I won't bore you with the details, but one weird occurrence in the fourth quarter is worth remembering since it still haunts me on occasion. I got a reasonably straightforward shot at goal to put us up 23-17, practically precisely where I'd landed a penalty a few minutes before. Donnybrook's flood lights turned on just as I was approaching. Not only that, but there was a bang - like a fuse blowing - just as I was about to strike the ball. I missed it. A few minutes later, they scored a try, and we lost 20-22.

I knew I'd made Dad proud, however. Coming off the pitch, I was upset, and I could tell he was too. I've seen that look on his face after past Schools Cup matches in which my brothers participated, when he was on the verge of tears - tears of agony and pride that myself, Mark, or Jerry had given everything we had.

And I noticed that expression on his face in Donnybrook that afternoon, as people milled around us outside the Bective clubhouse.

Chapter 4

This provides an overview of the pastoral care I got at St Mary's. I consider myself extremely lucky to have been influenced by instructors who were both dedicated to their jobs and concerned about their students.

A few things stand out from the letter. First, consider how prophetic it is. Some of Brian's cautions about professional athlete life have proven to be very accurate. But what startled me the most was Brian's underlying assumption that I would become a pro.

He doesn't appear to doubt that I was about to take this way. I wasn't quite convinced. At the very least, the individual at Leinster who made these decisions, Collie McEntee, did not appear very convinced of me.

McEntee was in charge of the newly established Leinster Academy. Until that moment, all of the best school-leavers had been invited to a centralized IRFU Academy, which held camps at various stages of the season. The goal of regionalizing the academy organization was to ensure that more players received more coaching and were assigned fitness programs that could be monitored more frequently.

I'd played for Leinster Schools for two years straight and attended all of the summer coaching camps. I was also very competitive and a terrible loser when it came to sports. I wanted to play at the highest potential level. I wanted to be a professional.

Failing to make the Ireland Schools squad had hurt, though. It felt as if I wasn't actually rated. It's not like Rob Kearney was rated.

There was no space for me in the Leinster academy, but McEntee did offer me a spot in the sub-academy. I wasn't exactly overwhelmed. These days, school-leavers will crawl over broken glass to get into our sub-academy; back then, I felt like an afterthought.

You were given a bursary at the academy, which was only a few thousand dollars but nonetheless recognized your potential as a professional. You also had the opportunity to train alongside full-time professionals on occasion.

My status may have risen if I had been chosen for the Ireland U19s trip to South Africa in March, three months before my examinations. I was not. There were a few trial matches versus England selections at the ALSAA site near Dublin Airport, but we weren't representing Ireland. We played in training tops.

I had almost lost interest. It was all about leaving now. Mary being knocked out of the cup meant I had a free run at my mock tests, which went really well. I received 550 points. If I could equal that in June, I'd be able to get into Medicine at UCD.

Many years later Ronan O'Gara called me Swot while I was racing. I never missed a single French class organized by the club for their foreign players. O'Gara would have liked to have seen me prepare for the Leaving. It's an exam method that typically rewards pupils who can process a large amount of knowledge and regurgitate it correctly on test day. This suited me perfectly.

I was fortunate in that I had good professors and was eager to work hard. I had Brian Wall for chemistry and math. He condensed each textbook's pertinent chapters to the essential stuff, which I memorized. Chemistry was factual and formulaic. You simply have to do the work. It was akin to math. I appreciated how it was process-oriented, with no grey spots. You had it right or wrong.

Having a specific goal helped me focus on my studies. Wherever possible, I'd stay overnight in Laura's spare room. She was not only my girlfriend, but also my tutor and financial support throughout our relationship. She was in her first year of university at the time, but on weekends she worked in a pub, delivering drinks and collecting glasses.

She was making a fortune between salaries and tips, so the few times we went out, whether to the movies or whatever, it was always her treat.

A less generous partner could have commented on my increasing weight. Once we were eliminated from the cup, my typical school day consisted of eating, studying, and sleeping. Not very healthy eating either. For breakfast, I'd generally get a bacon bun from the Spar near the school. During the mini-break at 11 a.m., the sixth-years had the school canteen to themselves, so it was chicken curry or sausage rolls and fries.

At lunchtime, we might go to Rathmines - Fast Food Central. Likewise after school. If I didn't have dinner at home, I might stop by the chipper six doors down for a cheeseburger.

I'm probably happy that the Irish Schools selectors hadn't seen me in a while when they put me in the squad for that August visit to Australia, which was a pleasant surprise. The seven-game tour culminated in a single 'Test' versus Australian Schools in Canberra.

I was usually quite reserved on tour. I was never comfortable sharing a room with a kid from another province until I got to know them. There were times during the trip when we were billeted with boys from opposing teams, which put even more strain on your social abilities. Now I know how beneficial it was for me. By now it was uncomfortable.

I was lucky to spend the Brisbane leg with Tony McGahan, who was coaching one of the local teams and would subsequently join the Munster coaching staff. Tony and his wife Libby had a wonderful house with a tiny room in the basement, where I dozed off with Peter Shallow, a kid from Rockwell College. I received the shock of my life when Tony appeared in his pajamas. He murmured, "I see you found my tapes." I was horrified, but he assured me not to worry. He ended up showing me a handful of his favorite attempts - two rugby nerds simply chewing the fat. Peter snored throughout.

I never made the Test team, but I gained confidence from the tour and Tony's gentle encouragement. He drove us about that week and saw us play against Queensland Schools. I remember getting right into it. I also scored a try after a fantastic show-and-go.

After the game, Tony approached me, looked me in the eyes, and said, "Mate, you can really play."

Looking back, it's strange how things turned out. Missing that question meant I missed out on studying medicine, but it also gave me a clearer path to playing professional rugby, as medical students suffer with time constraints. I was offered my second choice, chemical engineering at UCD. It was a poor decision in the end, but you live and learn.

He emailed me shortly after I returned from Australia, informing me that they'd be playing a pre-season friendly against Greystones in Kenilworth Square the next day and that I should come down to watch. I brought the dog down casually. Before halftime, I had made up my mind.

When I told Smythie I wanted to play for them, he seemed shocked. A school-leaver with aspirations to play professionally would typically join one of the institutions. But I admired the rugby Mary was attempting to play. I enjoyed the idea that there were so many guys on the squad who were years ahead of me in school, people I admired. Guys who were also capable of putting me in my place.

During my first training session, I tossed my IRFU-branded gear bag onto the bench in the first XV dressing room before heading for a leak. When I returned, my bag was gone. Dave Clare, the veteran loose-head prop and jail officer by trade, had thrown it into the parking lot. I had unwittingly taken his place, which amused everyone. An icebreaker, I suppose.

I kept giving them lots of entertainment. Our first AIL game took place in Limerick, versus Old Crescent. Since the provinces had been adequately professionalized, the league had lost much of its charm, and the spectators were no longer as large. However, there was no limit on the number of professionals permitted to play for their clubs, and the provinces had no A team matches yet. if a pro was fighting to have his contract renewed and needed to make his point, he'd do it in the MAIL. I recall Crescent having a few Munster players that day, including Mike Mullins, a former international, and Eoin Reddan.

The rugby was more violent than I was used to, but we won comfortably, with John McWeeney scoring a hat trick. This earned him the man of the match award. In the Crescent clubhouse, the MOTM has to stand on a stool and drink a pint in one go.

However, weekdays were tedious. It would begin with sub-academy fitness sessions at 6:30 a.m. In Belvo - Old Belvedere RFC, I used to cycle down with a bag of college books on my back. From there, I'd cycle to lectures at Earlsfort Terrace in town between 9 and 12 p.m. After that, I'd grab a ham and cheese roll before riding five kilometers to Belfield for additional classes from 2 to 5 p.m., followed by a ten-kilometer ride to Templeville for training, with a break for food at a service station along the way. It was crazy.

The lecturers told us that for every hour of lecture time, we should study for thirty minutes, which amounted to around three hours of study every day. This is on top of club training and the sub-academy. There were not enough minutes in the day.

My parents wanted me to take my academics seriously. They deliberately discouraged me from attending the sub-academy. It wasn't like I was being compensated for the privilege. By Christmas,

I had stopped showing up altogether. Leinster probably lost interest in me at that point.

My other difficulty was that I despised chemical engineering.

Thermodynamics and particle science? Ugh. By the end of the fall semester, I'd had enough. I broke down one night and told Mum that I couldn't go on.

I didn't want to leave college altogether. I still wanted a degree, but not in chemical engineering. I proposed switching to a Bachelor of Commerce and starting over the following September. People agreed, as long as I found work.

Steve Hennessy was able to assist us here. Steve worked for Friends First, a financial services company, and was able to secure me a position. Every morning on his way to work, Dad would drop me off at Steve's house around 7.50, and we'd go to the office in Cherrywood, where I'd spend the day evaluating loan applications from farmers wishing to purchase Massey Ferguson tractors, checking their credit ratings, and so on.

On training nights, Steve would take me to Templeville. We became good friends, despite the fact that I had to endure continual harassment in the locker room about being the coach's pet.

We played fantastic offensive rugby, but because the league was played in the dead of winter, I also learned how to control a game in the mud, wind, and rain, how to keep the forwards happy, and how to maintain a lead - all of which can only be learnt through experience.

Despite my desire to become a pro, I had no concept what professionalism entailed. My diet was still horrible, with tons of processed food in the canteen at Friends First and frequent late-night trips to the chipper in Rathgar. There was a dirty little weight room in Templeville, but I only went in for a show. The only reason I was in condition was because we did a lot of running after training, such as sprints and shuttle runs.

Smythie was aware of this as well, and privately informed me that he was pounding on the door at Leinster, telling them I was playing out of my skin.

Smythie and I were close friends that year. He lived fairly close to me at the time, and, more crucially, he subscribed to Sky Sports. I'd call him on a Sunday and ask if he was watching Leicester.

v. Northampton, and he'd invite me over and instruct me to pick up a sandwich at the deli across the street from my parents' house; his girlfriend Gillian worked there on weekends.

His unwavering passion for rugby and his extensive knowledge of the game amazed me. I consider myself a rugby fan, but Smythie was on another level. His professional career ended a few years ago when he underwent surgery to remove a golf ball-sized cancer inside his head.

The way to be noticed was to join the Ireland Under-21s.

Around Christmas 2004, Mark McDermott sent a squad of about forty players to Marcoussis to play two training games against French selections, and I was one of three outfield players, along with Gareth Steenson and Conan Doyle. This is despite not playing for the Leinster Under-21s in the interpros at the start of the season. It demonstrated that the AIL form still held some value.

I knew it would be difficult to move Steenson. He was the most obvious captain for the next U-21 Six Nations, having played in the team the previous season when Ireland defied the odds to reach the Junior World Cup final.

Sure enough, I did not make the initial Six Nations team, but when Steenson was injured, I was named to the bench for the game against

England at Donnybrook, with Munster's Barry Keeshan starting. I never got off the bench, but the fact that I was sitting there in my brand new IRFU tracksuit demonstrated that I had surpassed students who had been chosen ahead of me in the Schools setup. I was in the mix. What made it even better was that the game was held at Donnybrook, still Leinster's headquarters at the time. Someone would need to notice.

Mary kept presenting me with major days out in the spring of 2005, days where the media was present: a Division 1B final versus UL Bohs at Lansdowne Road, the Leinster Senior Cup final, and the new All-Ireland Cup Final. But the most essential goal of the season had been promotion to Division 1A, which we had achieved.

We also had a lot of fun. You were never allowed to take yourself too seriously at Mary's. Brian 'Rolo' Rowntree, the team manager, once asked me to do a television interview for RTÉ. I wasn't interested, but he emphasized that it would benefit the club game in Ireland and that they had requested me as an up-and-coming talent. Simply show up at RTÉ on Friday afternoon in your Mary's top, he instructed me. My only hope was that people would miss it because it was on afternoon TV. But, of course, Rolo made sure to record it and present it to the team. It took me a bit to get over it.

Mary knew how to keep your feet on the ground, but they also knew how to recognize individual accomplishments. They made a big deal about me when I was named to the Under-21s squad for the Junior World Cup in Argentina that summer.

Even better, Leinster recognized my efforts by enrolling me in the academy for the following season. It was almost as if they were forced to accommodate me, despite my disinterest in the sub-academy.

Collie McEntee sat me down before we left for Argentina and told me I'd have to do a massive pre-season to catch up on my physical development, and he cautioned me there would be no shortcuts.

I comforted him. I blamed my parents for my lack of attendance in sub-academy. It would be wonderful this time. I'd be back in college and wouldn't be hurrying to work at Friends First. I owned an automobile. It would be easy to attend every session.

Go ahead, good thing!

Argentina did well. Mendoza wasn't the most gorgeous location, but just being involved in an international event and competing for a starting slot was amazing. I could have sat back and accepted my place as backup out-half, knowing I'd be underage again the next season. But I figured I could put pressure on Steenson.

We had a decent team that included future senior internationals Stephen Ferris, Chris Henry, Kevin McLaughlin, and Andrew Trimble. During that tour, I developed a close friendship with Trimby. But we were in a tough pool and ended ninth, far lower than our pre-tournament position of second favourites. I was pleased with my contribution, which came primarily from the bench, as Gareth moved to 12. I got to start against Canada and Samoa and was pleased with how I performed.

The hard job began when we arrived home. Collie informed me that I needed to complete a twelve-week pre-season to catch up with my colleagues. Brad Harrington was waiting for me, and it quickly became clear that he was going to make me pay for all my missed workouts.

Brad was quite rough on me that summer in the Belvo gym. He was always on my case.

I kept hounding him, but he kept telling me I was on a specific program and wouldn't be able to play for another few weeks.

Besides, I had not yet trained with the team.

I begged him. If I could practice with them on Thursday and Friday, I'd be prepared for Saturday's Ulster game in Donnybrook.

He eventually succumbed, most likely due to fear of an interpro whitewash. I'd talked my way into the team.

I played like a dream, conceding a goal early on and hitting my wing with a well-weighted cross-kick. We killed them. Five minutes before the end, I was called ashore, pleasantly exhausted. I was slumped down at the side of the pitch, back against a hoarding with socks around my ankles, when I felt a tap on the shoulder.

'That was great, mate. 'See you at training on Monday,' said Michael Cheika, Leinster's new coach. Holy Christ.

I noticed the old man was down near the Bective end. Wait until he hears this.

Chapter 5

I remember 2009 as the happiest of times. It was the year I was air-dropped into a Heineken Cup semi-final at Croke Park, Leinster won Europe for the first time, and I made my international debut.

However, this was also the year I decided to leave Leinster.

Psychologists refer to 'negativity bias', which holds that negative experiences are more impactful than positive ones because they are more passionately felt and so more likely to be remembered. At the beginning of 2009, I was suffering from negativity bias and feeling really depressed. In January, I realized there was no way I was going to make it in Leinster. I contacted my agent, John Baker, to see what clubs would be interested in me. Worcester expressed some interest, but nothing came of it.

Our new house was essentially Cheiks' former office. It was rather cramped, but it was ours. More intimate, you may say. Established internationals were encouraged to sit alongside academy members and interact with them. Cheiks had actually written names on the wall above where he wanted people to sit. Younger players were placed between senior internationals. It helped us develop relationships.

This occurred in Round 2 of the Magners. I'm not sure how I got hit in the head, but I don't remember much about the rest of the day - and the little I do remember came back to me the next day in the form of flashbacks.

After the game, Laura is driving me out of the RDS. Brian pulls up alongside and asks how I am. He smiles as I attempt to communicate. Both of them appear delighted by my confusion, as neither of us had any idea how dangerous concussions were at the time. Brian then instructs Laura to make sure I'm okay.

Aside from this clip, I rely on other people's accounts of what occurred. Brian and Felipe informed me that I was speaking gibberish on the pitch, making calls they'd never heard before.

Laura was there, which surprised me because she used to stay with her folks the night before a game. She attempted to describe what had happened the night before. Apparently, I needed some convincing.

If a player has a concussion like this currently, he is hospitalized overnight for observation. Back then, the guidelines were a little looser.

Laura had come down to the dressing room area to get me. She was instructed to keep an eye on me, not to allow me drive, and to notify the team doctor if I felt ill.

If you were injured, you were supposed to report for a medical checkup the day following the game. But you wouldn't have highlighted a concussion back then. It probably meant you'd be stood down for two weeks, and I didn't want to give Cheiks an excuse to do so.

When reporters asked Cheiks why I had been removed so early, he stated I had received a 'boost', which was not questioned. He stood me down for the following week, instead starting Isa against the Dragons.

We had another heated argument after training on Tuesday following the concussion. Cheiks clearly noticed my dissatisfaction and politely inquire whether everything was fine. I would have been on the defensive, as I often was at the time, hearing criticism in every word. Conversation quickly degenerated to confrontation.

His fundamental advice, as I recall, was to stay positive and not get discouraged, as I had done when I was replaced in those pre-season games.

My interactions with Cheeks were not always confrontational. He dedicated a lot of time to instructing me. He used to show me grainy old films of the Ella brothers and other Randwick teammates following the pass and looking for a second or third touch.

On the one hand, I appreciated the knowledge he was providing me and paid close attention. On the other hand, I interpreted it as criticism. He was showing me stuff that I wasn't doing. Looking back, I wish I had known what I know now. After working with some outstanding coaches and sports psychologists later in my career, I realized I wasted a lot of time and energy being too sensitive and insecure, rather than having a development mentality and motivation to improve day after day.

Isa fractured his arm against the Ospreys, which sidelined him for a few months and gave me an opportunity. But I wasn't in the best psychological shape, and I certainly wasn't prepared to face Munster, who returned to the RDS the following week determined to get revenge. The sight of Rocky and CJ making their Leinster debuts fueled their enthusiasm even further.

It ended with Leinster 0, Munster 18 - our first defeat in the RDS in twelve months, and the first time I heard 'The Fields of Athenry' sung there. This was not a good experience.

The newspapers did not make for easy reading, either. Gerry Thornley of the Irish Times hailed O'Gara's performance highly, writing that I had been 'pedestrian by comparison'. Neil Francis of the Sunday Tribune claimed that my performance was 'below AIL standard'. Nice.

I read everything written about me. Not only would I scour the newspapers, but I'd also type my name into search engines and sift through fans' internet communities, hoping for nice references and fearing bad ones. I knew nothing better. I wasn't the only person doing it. It's natural to want to know what people are saying and writing about you. However, it can fry your brain.

I could demonstrate self-awareness to a journalist, but could I follow through and give myself a break? Not when results went against me. The week after Munster, I started against Connacht in Galway, and we lost, rekindling old fears about our vulnerability. When Felipe came in for the first Heineken game, away to Edinburgh, everything clicked. The following week, we won another bonus-point game at home against Wasps, with Felipe starting at 10.

At least I contributed positively off the bench against Wasps. With my initial touch, I sent Luke to the left corner with a beautiful pass. That night, I watched it on tape and replayed that moment several times.

Sky Sports' Will Greenwood called it ' magical, an absolutely magnificent piece of talent by the replacement, Kearney'.

The following week, I started my journey to Glasgow. We lost. I took comfort in the idea that Deccie had included me in the November international training team, which would provide me with vital experience. Furthermore, Felipe was no longer able to work due to a serious hand infection. With Isa still healing, I had a decent opportunity of getting my first Heineken start when we faced Castres back-to-back in December.

I was still troubled by misgivings, persuaded that Checks did not truly believe in me. This was only exacerbated when he flew David Holwell in from New Zealand as short-term out-half cover. Holwell has been a Leinster fan favorite. Was he a threat? Of course, he was.

Cheiks put him on the bench for the first Castres game, at the RDS, and he replaced me in the final quarter. It seemed like the crowd was applauding Holwell onto the pitch a lot louder than they were applauding me off it.

We won that game by 30 points but failed to secure a four-try bonus point, so it was reported almost as a failure. The media abuse was only starting, though. When we lost in Castres the following Friday night, the flak really flew. Leinster 'ladyboys' – all that stuff.

I'm tempted to absolve myself of guilt here, seeing as we were leading 12–9 when Cheiks gave me the hook. At half-time! I'd just scored a try and I'd played pretty well in general, barring one sloppy missed conversion. But this was Felipe's first game back after the hand infection and I'm guessing Cheeks had decided he was going to give him the second forty, regardless. He just came into the dressing room and said: 'Phil, you're on. Johnny, you're off.'

He started talking about where we needed to improve. I heard none of it. I felt like I'd been winded. Devastated.

That was probably the night I decided I was quitting Leinster. This might sound like me being unreasonable, over-emotional. I was still not established, whereas Felipe had been nominated for World Player of the Year only twelve months previously. It still felt unfair.

I'd never been replaced at half-time, in any team. And it had been done so casually.

Phil, you're on. Johnny, you're off. The humiliation.

As I sat frozen in the stands for the second half, I was wondering where I would go play my rugby next year, and half-rooted for Castres. They'd already lost at home five times that season, but they had some decent players and they sniffed an opportunity to win back some respect from their supporters. Meanwhile, we were awful, off the pace. Castres 18, Leinster 15.

He told us about how he'd choked on the final hole of the British Open the previous year only to be rescued by his caddy, Ronan

Flood. Standing on the seventy-second tee at Carnoustie, he led Sergio García by a shot. But he drove his tee shot into the Barry Burn and then knocked his third into the water at the front of the green.

'When I hit the second ball in the water, I just died there,' he told us. 'I just felt embarrassed. I felt I'd thrown away the Open.'

As he walked down towards the drop-zone, he allowed himself to imagine his father's disappointment, to imagine the disappointment of Irish people watching in pubs and golf clubs all over the country.

Flood had kept at him, though, bombarding him with positive thoughts. Screw your head on, Pádraig. You've a pitch from forty-five metres. Get up and down for a 6 and you've a good chance of being in the play-off. And of course, Harrington won that play-off with García.

You assume these superstars are bulletproof mentally, but this made me realize that they aren't. They've won majors and yet they're fragile. They're human. I'd had those doubts on the pitch, especially as a place-kicker. And I let them influence me. It felt like he was speaking directly to me.

From that point on, he'd decided to pay no attention to the media.

He told his wife he didn't want to hear what was being said about him.

Again, this chimed with me. I wasn't good at dealing with criticism, whether it was from Cheeks or the media. When it was criticized with no basis in fact, it infuriated me.

You've no idea how uplifting it was to discover that one of my sporting heroes had suffered from such doubts and insecurities. It felt like a real turning point – my first insight into the thinking of an elite sportsman. It sparked an interest in sports psychology. The following week, I went out and bought Golf is not a Game of Perfect by Harrington's sports psychologist, Bob Rotella.

For all the encouragement I was getting in Camp Ireland, January 2009 found me in a strange place. Essentially I was one injury away from featuring in the Six Nations – a scary state of affairs when you consider the only rugby I was getting was in the MAIL. Deccie was blessed that O'Gara stayed fit for the entirety of that season.

Here's another way of looking at it. Between 12 December and 21 February, I didn't play a single second for Leinster, despite being fully fit. No wonder I was looking to leave. The club had offered me a new two-year deal at €100K, so clearly they saw me as part of their future. I couldn't see my future at Leinster.

Cheiks now had everybody on board. Isa, Felipe and Darce were all fit again. Cheiks started Isa at 10 for five straight games before realizing he had more to offer in the back three. I trained with the squad all week, running with the bibs, or I was in Ireland camp, again running with the bibs. The weekends I spent with Mary's.

At least the early finish meant I'd definitely get back to the apartment in time to watch the game at Twickenham. Kev McLaughlin and Ross McCarron came. We ordered pizzas and settled in to watch the demise of Cheiks.

That's how this game was being viewed. If Leinster lost, their chances of qualifying were effectively gone. And if they didn't qualify, Cheiks was gone.

Myself, Kev and Ross were all in the same boat: disaffected, feeling victimised and hoping Wasps won. We still have a laugh about it among ourselves and exaggerate the details – how we were sitting there with Wasps flags, wearing yellow and black face-paint. Complete traitors, sworn conspirators. But part of me did want Leinster to fail.

Instead, Leinster won with a bonus point, and secured qualification to the knockout stages by beating Edinburgh the next week.

The day before that Edinburgh game, I'd been playing for Mary's in Belvo. There were so few people watching that I had no difficulty spotting Cheiks leaning on the railing behind the posts at one end. When I kicked a touchline conversion in front of him, to seal Mary's win, I resisted the urge to say something to him.

My plan was to make my point against the England Saxons at Donnybrook – Deccie had picked me in the A team, even though a few people had been calling for Ian Humphreys to get a run. I felt cheated when the game was abandoned due to a frozen pitch.

Deccie came into the dressing room to commiserate with me, which I appreciated.

At this stage it was out there that I had itchy feet. The Irish Sun even ran a story linking me to Perpignan, which was news to me! I'd received supportive phone calls from team-mates. Leo and Jenno urged me to be patient. They said we were a good team with me at 10, that my chance would come.

I spent hours on the phone with Bernard Jackman, who suggested I email Cheiks to let him know my frustrations. I didn't feel comfortable doing that. I really appreciated the gestures of support from my team-mates, but the paranoid me suspected that Checks had put them up to it.

When he called, I basically told him that I loved Leinster but that I didn't want to hold tackle-bags for the rest of my life. He told me he wanted me to stay and reassured me there would be opportunities. This was good to hear but I committed to nothing just yet.

I replaced Girve with thirty minutes to go, at which stage we trailed 9–0. In other words, we still hadn't scored a point against Munster that season, in two hours of trying. I was desperate to shake things up. Within minutes of arriving, I was stuck into a shouting match with Shaggy. No idea what it was about.

The real flare-up started when I went to clear out Lifeimi Mafi after he'd tip-tackled Chris Whitaker. I caught him above the eye with a stud by accident and he retaliated. A few fists were thrown.

Paul O'Connell was quick on the scene, asking Mafi who'd caused the gash above his eye. Suddenly I have Paulie pointing the finger at me and giving me a mouthful. A scary sight. I squared my shoulders at him, but from a safe distance.

I think Cheiks was impressed too. I was given a two-week suspension for reckless use of my studs, but he still brought me to the Stoop for the infamous 'Bloodgate' Heineken quarter-final against Harlequins, where I acted as water-boy and message-carrier. Johnny O'Hagan's assistant, basically.

Even with another strong impression off the bench against Glasgow the week before Croker, I wasn't confident of making the twenty-two. With Isa in the back three, Cheiks had cover for out-half and Rob had been flying at full-back – already an established international, and he'd been selected for the Lions tour to South Africa that summer. But he'd been flattened by mumps after the quarter-final and wasn't ready for the semi. His misfortune was my first big break.

Smythie had said it to me a few times: Your chance will come. When it does, make sure you're ready. After Harrington's talk I had a new mindset. I had started to meet regularly with Enda McNulty. We worked together for hours on my routine. He would throw in all sorts of distractions and scenarios. We spoke about visualizing big moments in a European final. Still, you never think that it will be twenty-five minutes into the biggest club game in Irish rugby history, at Croke Park in front of a crowd of 82,300, in a Heineken Cup semi-final, against the reigning champions, with the entire country tuned in.

You definitely don't imagine that your first act will be to kick at goal. Or that you'll be kept waiting about two minutes to take that kick, with your knees shaking. Literally.

Felipe was coming off, having slipped awkwardly on his knee. My second big break. As I'm waiting for the nod to replace him, I'm wondering: Do the laws allow a replacement to take a shot at goal as his first act? I'm half-hoping they don't. Then Isa will have to take it. But no. It's me. OK. Where's my tee?

Usually, having Johnny O'Hagan on tee-duty was a blessing. A familiar face. A kind face. A face from my childhood. This time, it's a half-apologetic face. He has three tees in his hand – orange, red, green. I think the match-day organizers used the green one to perch a Heineken-branded ball near the entry to the tunnel and Hago had just grabbed it. However, he doesn't have MY green tee. He's mixed them up. This is a problem.

Don't think about the fact that on this beautifully warm Saturday afternoon, the entire country is tuned into this sporting civil war, and Croker is jammed, with rival fans corralled into massive blocks of blue and red. Don't think about the fact that all of them are looking at me.

Luckily, it never occurred to me at the time that this was my first 'live' place-kick in nearly three months, since that game against Scotland A.

I hadn't place-kicked for Leinster because that was Felipe's gig. At Mary's, it was usually Barry Lynn. I had been practising, though.

Hago had told my old man on the QT that he'd heard the coaching

46

staff saying that I wasn't reliable enough off the tee. So I'd done lots of sessions with Enda and with Richie Murphy. I'd even done the occasional session with Dave Alred, the kicking guru then best known at that time for his work with Jonny Wilkinson. Paul Moloney in Adidas Ireland had set it up for me.

All three – Richie, Enda and Dave – had shown me the importance of formulating a routine that I would stick to, rigidly, for every kick.

It's amazing to think that I was only getting around to this at the age of twenty-three. These days, kids have got this nailed before they're playing Junior Cup. I'd spent hours honing the process.

The final scoreline was 25–6. This was a massive upset. Munster had already thumped us twice that season, and had crushed Ospreys in the quarters. Eight of their players had been selected to tour South Africa with the Lions, compared to four of ours: Rob, Luke, Brian and Jamie. Munster had been almost unbackable favourites to retain the Heineken.

But that was the day when we finally delivered on our potential, the day our pack really stepped forward, the day when Rocky Elsom became a cult hero – although he had been exceptional at the Stoop also, and would be brilliant again in the final. Sometimes you wonder if the reason he's such a legend with Leinster supporters is because he was only here for one memorable season. Then you look at some of his clips and you realize he was freakishly good. He barely trained, as he was managing his body through consecutive northern and southern hemisphere seasons. He only spoke when he needed to. But when it mattered, he delivered. Put it this way: I don't think we'd have won the Heineken Cup without him.

At this stage, I'm actually glad I did. I was just being me.

I know it wasn't a great example for the thousands of kids who were watching. I'm not sure how I'd feel about my kids seeing it, or how

I'll explain it to them when the time comes. But stuff like this happens in competitive sports. And was it really that bad? His words had played over and over in my head for weeks building up to this game. 'You're useless, nobody.'

During the lockdown, I watched some old GAA reruns on TV and what I did was nothing compared to some of the stuff that went on in hurling and football. And those lads were celebrated for their passion.

Besides, I went to O'Gara at the final whistle and offered my hand. He told me to fuck off. He had the hump, big-time. Maybe it had something to do with the fact that Brian had intercepted him for our final try.

He must have cooled down a bit by the time he came into our dressing room to congratulate his Leinster buddies, Brian and Shaggy. He still made sure to give me the death-stare on his way out. I was sitting in one of the subs' spots, near the door, and he paused just long enough to let me know I was in his bad books.

We went to the town that night with girlfriends, wives and partners. Almost everyone we met asked me what I'd said to O'Gara. I have no idea what words came out of my mouth or whether they were remotely coherent. I'm sure it was just a roar.

At one point we bumped into Les Kiss, who was coaching both of us in the Ireland set-up. Even he said he'd been delighted to see me 'put it up to Rog'. But I cringed a bit when I saw the papers the next morning. I had managed to take Pádraig Harrington's advice on board and would not read a word, but the picture was everywhere. I knew it was going to cause me grief.

Felipe had actually helped put me in a positive mood.

He told me to concentrate on what I could do to help the team, rather than agonize over personal performance. Simple? A lot of the best advice is. And I appreciated Felipe taking the time to talk to me. Our relationship was always excellent, but for him it must have been devastating to miss this game. He had brought us here and now he was missing.

I was pretty confident anyway. The week after Munster, we'd smashed the Scarlets at the RDS, 45–8. I'd place-kicked well and scored a try from forty metres out.

In Edinburgh, we stayed at the Dalmahoy, a palatial country club.

In eve-of-match meetings, there's usually not much pressure on younger guys to contribute. But the 10 is a leader by definition, so I said my piece in the dressing room:

We have to believe that this is our year. We have to believe it's scripted for us. Look at the way we were written off post-Castres, the way we defended for our lives in Harlequins, the way we beat the reigning champions at Croker. This is our year – but we have to start believing it.

I was probably fortunate that Kev McLaughlin wasn't there to remind me that only a few months previously, we'd been rooting for Wasps to knock Leinster out of the tournament, or that I'd been trying to leave the club. I'd forgotten all that.

I was grand once I got to the stadium. It helped that I'd played there before. It also helped that Murrayfield was mostly coloured blue. We'd read all the interviews with Munster players who'd gone on about their supporters taking ownership of Cardiff when they'd played finals at the Millennium Stadium. Well, now it was our turn.

When we were walking the pitch, Stan Wright gave me a pat on the back and muttered something about me having nothing to worry about. Given that Stan rarely said anything to anyone who wasn't a front rower, I reckoned he must have been worried on my behalf.

This was only my third start in a Heineken Cup match, after all. The lads were used to having Felipe there but Felipe was in his suit, hobbling around on crutches.

But I was fine. I usually am, once I get to the ground. Time to get on with it.

I had a good first touch, which helped. It was the first touch of the match, in fact – a kick-off aimed at Geordan Murphy that hung in the air long enough for our chasers to wrap him up. Geordan was their go-to man for clearances so it had been the plan to deny him that chance. A positive start.

Young players thrown into a sporting cauldron often go out with the intention to 'keep things simple' to reduce the chances of making an error. Battling with this is an impulse to announce yourself, to make an impression. That day in Edinburgh, around eighteen minutes into the contest, the impulse took over.

As I was running back, allowing myself a celebratory fist-pump, Stuart Barnes was gushing on Sky: 'That is a wonderful kick from the twenty-three-year-old. He's made such a composed start. That's a pure strike.'

Confidence surged through me. I found other ways to assert myself. Because Leicester were using a rush defence on Brian, passing to him was rarely an option, so I was effectively forced into attacking the 12 channel. I was fine with that. I had a dart, offloaded to Dance with my left hand. He didn't get over but it was only a matter of inches.

We were all over them. And yet the Tigers led 13–9 at the break.

Having defended like dogs, they made the most of their period of dominance at the end of the half, at which stage we were down to fourteen men after Stan had taken Sam Vesty out off the ball. Soon Vesty's offload put Ben Woods over and we were trailing for the first time. Leicester's lead became 16–9 when Julien Dupuy landed a penalty early in the second half.

We always looked likely to finish stronger, given that we'd all had the previous weekend off, when the Tigers had been on Premiership duty. They had English and French internationals to bring off the bench, but our scrum held up brilliantly. At the lineout, we had the advantage of Leo and Jenno's insider knowledge. We made it count.

It still came down to a penalty shot, ten minutes from the end, thirty-five metres out on the left-hand side. Out came Hago with the tee, and some advice from Richie: Stay tall and strike through the target. It wasn't the purest strike. In fact it was pretty ugly, starting off well right of the posts but then hooking back on the breeze. I knew from the warm-up and Dupuy's penalty in the first half that it would move right to left. It had just enough on it. Watch the tape and you see me giving Richie a knowing smile as I run back. It almost looks like I'm enjoying myself.

Ten minutes later, I'm distraught. Nigel Owens has blown for a breakdown penalty against us and it's just about in kickable range. I'm forty metres away with my head in my hands. Then I realize it's a peno for us. I run over and Chris Whitaker tosses me the ball to bog into the stands. It's over.

I was engulfed by some of the younger squad members, guys like Paulie O'Donohoe and Eoin O'Malley, then Richie. Little Jerry tried to get me, too, and got in a bit of bother with the stewards. He was only sixteen at the time and with a few beers inside him, he decided he couldn't wait to congratulate me. I had a word with one of the high-vizzers and so we got to have a boozy, brotherly hug.

This had been a long journey and I'd played a relatively small part in it. For some senior players, it was their tenth Heineken Cup campaign. Brian paid tribute to the Denis Hickies, Victor Costellos, Reggie Corrigans, guys who'd given so much to the Leinster cause, who'd put up with the abuse during the dark days. Leo forced Chris Whitaker to accept the cup with him. Typically, Whits didn't want to take centre stage but we knew this was his final appearance for the club so Leo wouldn't take no for an answer.

As we did our lap of honour, draped in Leinster scarves and hats and flags, with U2 blaring and so many familiar faces in the stands, it occurred to me how mad this outcome was – how low I'd been in the dressing room in Castres only a few months previously, how ecstatic I was now. And then I just stopped thinking and let happiness wash over me.

Chapter 6

Leinster and Joe Schmidt met at just the right time. We were hungry, having stewed all summer after losing a home final to the Ospreys and being eliminated in a European semi-final.

Joe was ambitious, having only served as an assistant coach up until that moment. He was possibly also the coach I had subconsciously been looking for: someone who believed in me from the start and trusted me totally.

The Joe-Johnny friendship has entertained the boys over the years. They used to nickname me the teacher's pet. They claim Joe is my long-lost father, my true father. But Joe's trust was gained. It took a while to find his wavelength and figure him out.

All this information was reduced into a list of favorable attributes.

Then he asked us to identify the six players who best exemplified those attributes. When the scores' were tallied, Joe had effectively established his leadership group. I was included. We met with him that evening to discuss the distillation process further. After a few hours, we had distilled everything into three words: humble, disciplined, and ruthless. These were the standards by which we might hold ourselves accountable.

I was worried about the humility issue. Someone had mentioned that there might be a negative perception of us out there, that we regarded ourselves too highly simply because we had won one Heineken Cup. And Joe had leaped on it. Perhaps he was wary of our team's star culture.

We had a poor start to the league, thanks in part to the internationals being gradually reintroduced into the squad. We lost three of our first four games. We even lost Treviso, being the first Irish team to do so. Joe rinsed in the media. I recall calling him to reassure him that we were behind him. What he was doing was going to be good. We simply needed everyone to get fit and onto the pitch.

Stephen was a popular part of the squad and a valuable presence in the locker room. People were irritated to hear he was being fired, but it also caused everyone to sit up and pay attention. It did not matter how popular you were.

We were encouraged to speak up in meetings, but if Joe didn't agree with you, he cut you off with a single syllable: Nah.

It was devastating.

Joe, I think we should have a runner coming short here... Nah. We do not need to do that.

Joe, last season we did X. Nah.

The good news was that he'd explain why X didn't work. I enjoyed the clarity and assurance he was providing us. You make suggestions to some instructors, and even if they disagree with you, they will not express it directly. They'll give you a vague explanation to keep you on board. Joe had a good and wrong manner of doing things, and you knew which was which. As an out-half, this is what you desire. You want every player in the squad to be on the same page.

He educated and entertained us, whether he realized it or not. Anyone who had received the Joe treatment in a meeting was also given a thorough examination in the dressing room. Someone took one of those Leinster baseball caps and pasted a sticker with the word 'NAH' over the emblem. Anyone who was burned by Joe in a meeting had to wear the headgear during training.

People slagged me. Joe never burns the teacher's pet, they remarked. That was due to my keen attention to detail. I've finished my assignment.

Joe's sole complaint about me that autumn was that I had hurt my kicking quad again. I had invited Dave Alred over for a session early in the season and may have gone overboard. I didn't play until the Munster game in early October, and it was just for twenty minutes off the bench, with no place kicks. At the very least, I got a feel for the Aviva, which had recently opened. We won, too. That made it five straight.

I wasn't ready to kick against Racing the next week, but Joe still wanted me to play, which delighted me much. We witnessed the level of his preparation that week. He made profiles of the Racing players and posted them on the wall of our conference room. He demonstrated how Andrea Masi was a man-watcher in defense and how susceptible he was to a wraparound by myself and Brian. We attempted it shortly before the break, and it worked great, with Rob finishing in the left corner. We sliced them open several times and ended up outscoring them five to one.

Until we arrived to face the Springboks, and the place was only two-thirds filled. The IRFU eventually confirmed that they had overcharged its tickets that autumn. It was 2010. People were broke. The place seemed dead. To make matters worse, our unique commemorative jerseys were quickly ripped apart, forcing us to change them at halftime. Plus, we lost 21-23.

It was no shame to lose to the world champs, especially since we were missing Paulie. But we had not played well. The goal was to shift away from the confined game plan that had won a Slam and widen our attacking alternatives. On a damp evening, our execution was inadequate.

I didn't play poorly, but with fifteen minutes left, we were behind 9–23, and Deccie had to make changes. Typically, on his hundredth cap, O'Gara seized the opportunity. We scored two tries before the end, and he assisted in both. He attempted a convert to tie the score, but it deflected off the upright.

I was probably not in the mood to perform a Q&A in one of the gleaming new corporate boxes after the game, but it's part of the job. At least I knew who was asking the questions: Fred Cogley, a former TV analyst who had done some media training with us in the academy and was Mary's man. I wasn't prepared for his inquiry, "Well, Jonathan, what about that masterclass from Ronan O'Gara?" despite his previous advice to prepare for difficult questions.

Maybe that was intended to be a joke, but I don't recall anyone laughing. I offered a straight bat and complemented Ronan, as you do. I got out of there as quickly as I could.

I was relieved when Deccie decided to start me against the All Blacks. And nervous, considering what had transpired in New Plymouth. This time, we lost 18-38 but did not feel too horrible about ourselves. That's simply a reflection of where we were in 2010 and where they were.

The opening forty was the best I'd had in eleven appearances for Ireland. We took the game to them, playing with traditional aggression while also displaying width and variation. The Aviva also responded, and it was heaving on this particular occasion. But then the All Blacks answered. We were leading 13-12 going into the interval, but they upped the ante on their recycling game, eventually breaking us. We staggered back to the changing room, and I vomited in the jacks. I had never encountered such intensity before.

Dad was already in Listowel, with his four brothers. He said the casket would be kept open for me if I could make it down by Tuesday night; it was a traditional country funeral with a two-day wake. I left with Laura after training. It wasn't until we were in town that the feeling struck me.

Daddy John's coffin had been on the counter in the William Street shop for two days by that point, as the passageway into the sitting room was too tiny to move it through. Many people had passed to pay their respects. There were tears, stories, laughter, jokes. My relatives were having a good time winding up this fellow who was at the coffin paying his respects. They kept phoning Daddy John's phone, which was in the casket with him, just to see how the man reacted. Will he answer the phone? This had them in stitches. Then the emotion took control again.

They buried Daddy John with his phone and a deck of cards. He used to call you when it was calm in the shop. He was very chatty with my mother and Laura. I loved staying in contact with folks. And now, the next day, we were strolling behind his hearse all the way from the church to the graveyard on the Ballybunion Road, halting at the shop where he had spent his entire life, with the entire town at a standstill. It was the week before Christmas, and it was chilly. I remember because all I was wearing was a suit. I caught a cold but was determined to play the return game against Clermont at the Aviva on Saturday. We won convincingly, but I was overtaken with emotion in the dressing room afterwards. Grief can manifest itself at unexpected times.

I missed Leinster's Christmas party a few nights later. I was on a secret, pre-arranged expedition to Paris, where Cheiks was showing me around his new club, Stade Français. He had made offers to me and Seánie.

I'm joking when I suggest the mission was kept secret. I hoped to be discovered. I left my phone on so that when team members called to ask why I wasn't at the party, they would hear the foreign telephone tone and rumors could spread. It may sound juvenile, but contract negotiations with the IRFU were frequently turned into a game.

We were almost through February when Deccie inquired where it was. I informed him that, considering O'Gara's expertise and accomplishments, I didn't expect to be on the same pay scale as him, but I did want my income to reflect my position in the hierarchy. He gave me no reason to believe I was being unreasonable.

It was subsequently decided that I'd receive large bonuses for each Six Nations appearance that year. I was relieved to get things sorted. I had no wish to leave Leinster, of course. Joe Schmidt helped me appreciate my profession like never before. We blew Saracens aside in Round 5 and then blasted Racing in Paris, where I scored a pair of tries and 21 points - perfect timing with the Six Nations looming. We won our pool and secured a home quarter-final against Leicester following the Six Nations.

Probably for the first time in my career, I felt entirely at ease playing for Leinster because I knew the coach trusted my decision. I enjoyed how he thought about the game. He would push us to attack space from any position on the pitch. 'If it's on, get your backs ready.' If I sprinted from my own try line, delivered a pass to the edge, and the guy dropped it, it was his fault, not mine. Joe instructed with such clarity that I could hear his voice in my brain throughout the games. Chasing space no matter where you are on the field. He was going to support me every time.

Out-half is certainly the position where you most need to feel like you have the coach's confidence. You are his quarterback. You are in a different connection with him. Maybe some men need to feel some heat to perform at their best, but if the out-half is looking over his shoulder, wondering if he'll play each week, he can't successfully lead the team. That was my main problem with Ireland at the time.

Deccie had excellent technical trainers in Les, Gert Smal, and Riff, and Merv's analysis was always top-notch. However, when we discussed expanding our attacking approach, I had the impression that Deccie was hesitant to move the ball from deep positions. We certainly needed to improve our attacking game if we were to compete at the World Cup, however. We had many offensive talents. However, our rocky start to the Six Nations exacerbated our lack of confidence.

First, we had a near escape in Rome, where O'Gara came off the substitute to grab the win with a late drop-goal. You have to give it to him. It was a fantastic moment for him, and it put the emphasis back on me.

I was suddenly filled with doubt again. It didn't help that Brian dug me up in the video review. He dropped my pass at one point throughout the game, claiming it was 'unsympathetic'. Apparently, I had taken too much out of the ball. I needed to offer it earlier. From where I sat, it appeared that he was blaming me for dropping the ball. In that situation, I lacked the confidence to challenge the skipper. Instead, I boxed up my grievance and allowed it to fester.

The next week, we fell 22-25 to France in Dublin. We placed more balls on the floor and had poor discipline, but I thought I played well. Riff told reporters he was happy for me. So did Deccie. He still dropped me off for the trip to Edinburgh.

'I felt Jonathan had a great game, but Ronan has also been playing really well,' he told the media. 'Not everyone who wants a game gets one, but I believe Ronan deserves one, which is why he's getting a start.'

When we chatted in person, I didn't get anything out of him. In that case, the athlete seeks advice on where they might improve, but Deccie stated that he was satisfied with me. He would have preferred me to kick rather than run from deep once against France, when we gave the ball over at halfway. I thought it was time to go, and being rolled over wasn't an issue. I was hoping Joe would have investigated why we turned the ball over. Looking back, I should not have been so sensitive to negative input, but when you know you're going to be cut from the team as a result, it's difficult to take it as constructive.

Deccie claimed he wasn't blaming me. Nonetheless, he must have believed that Ronan was a safer pair of hands for a game he needed to win. Or maybe Deccie simply wanted to keep things competitive at 10.

Competition might help you stay sharp. But you don't want to feel like you're going to be dismissed because of terrible outcomes from potentially good decisions. That way, you don't know if you're coming or going. The message I received was that he did not trust me to do the task at Murrayfield.

We nearly didn't. O'Gara was man of the match, scoring one of our three tries, but we were only up six points when I substituted him with twelve minutes remaining. That had been reduced to three points by the end, when we were fighting for our life. When I hoofed the ball into the stands to end the suffering, O'Gara raced onto the field to celebrate, and we exchanged an awkward hug.

I had conflicting feelings: delighted to have won, of course, but frustrated that I hadn't been able to direct us to safety with more authority. My mood only got darker as I turned on my phone. It was buzzing, primarily with remarks regarding RTÉ pundit George Hook. He had apparently gone on a rage, stating that Deccie should not start me again until the World Cup game against Russia. Great.

I came on as a substitute against Wales in Cardiff with 30 minutes remaining. We led 13-9 at the time, but I began like a man unsure of himself. My error resulted in a highly controversial Welsh try.

When I gathered the ball around my own 22-yard line, my impulse was to run.

It was on. But I had a million other thoughts going through my head. I kicked because I was torn between two ideas. Badly. I cut it into touches. However, the trouble was only beginning.

Matthew Rees, the Wales hooker, threw a fast pass to Mike Phillips, who snuck in from the corner. Rees threw the wrong ball from the wrong spot, hence the try should not have been allowed. But the referee and touch judge agreed it was alright. James Hook converted the try, making it a seven-pointer.

We wound up losing by six. Sickener.

To make matters worse, I missed a highly kickable penalty near the end. Regardless, I found some comfort. As we pursued the game in the fourth quarter, I sensed a spark, a good charge. It could have been an exchange with Paulie. We considered kicking to the corner at one point, but my line-kick barely made it into the Welsh 22, and he told me how he felt about my effort. The next time we attempted it, I spiraled it into the corner. Receiving his seal of approval made me feel a million bucks.

We did not score. I'm not sure how the Welsh kept us out, but they did. With England on track for a Grand Slam in Dublin, we were in danger of finishing in the bottom half of the table.

No doubt I received a lot of media criticism for two major mistakes, but to be fair to Deccie, he saw all my strengths and picked me to start against England. I felt I had something to prove, and I was irritable all week. It felt like everyone was on my side, and everyone had an opinion. No matter how hard you try, you can't ignore everything that has been reported in the media. In the team room, I noticed a headline over an article on the back page of the paper that mentioned me being the 'wrong' out-half for the Irish back row. It was nonsense, but it drew additional attention. I'd never had an encounter like this before.I was prepared to depart. So was he. Red mist covers both sides. Darce had to intervene and separate us. We were inches from a full-scale punch-up. Even when things calmed down and we resumed running plays, it felt like it could start again at any moment. When we finished, we parted ways.

I was aware that I had acted inappropriately. I texted Brian that night to explain and apologize for being disrespectful. He expressed appreciation for the text and said he should have called me. We hugged it out the next morning.

Our tiny outburst set the tone for the week and the match.

Were England going to win a Grand Slam? On our patch? Deccie got things going smoothly in the build-up. Brian and Paulie did the same thing.

I didn't need any more stirring. I was so fed up with all the negativity around me that I felt no pressure at all. I just wanted to go outside. That week, I made the conscious decision that I didn't care what happened in the game. I was simply going to play what I saw, trust myself, and go for it. When we received an early penalty at our own 22, I tapped and ran. We made it seventy metres and the crowd was ecstatic.

I was buzzing. Focused enough to land three first-half penalties as our pack took control, but aggressive in everything I did. Soon, I was given the choice of a fourth, but I could see England had turned off, so I tapped again and put Tommy in for a try.

Nine minutes after the interval, Brian scooped for his twenty-fifth championship try, beating the previous record. I was the first to hug. When I converted from the left touchline, we were up 24-3. It was Ireland's best performance.

Ten minutes before the finale, the audience gave me a good send-off.

Someone in the TV world had determined I was man of the match. When Tracy Piggott of RTÉ interviewed me on the pitch, I smiled and resisted the impulse to hammer it into everyone who had been on my case. In the mixed zone, the media inquired about my relationship with O'Gara. Naturally.

'What occurs on the pitch between Munster and Leinster goes out the window when we arrive at the Irish camp,' I added. 'I'm sure in a few weeks we'll be back killing each other in Thomond, but we're great friends today and as we build up to the World Cup.'

Poor Richie Hughes was unable to watch any longer. At halftime, he went for a walk and turned off the phone. Later, he told me that he had strolled down to Rathfarnham's Church of the Annunciation to light a few candles because we definitely needed some inspiration. Fortunately, he turned his phone back on as he arrived outside the church and received a flurry of SMS telling him to get home. Leinster were making a comeback!

I didn't feel like I was saying anything particularly amazing in the dressing room, just what was on my mind.

I was seething because I knew the scoreboard was deceptive.

Yes, we had missed a few tackles, and yes, we needed to work on the scrum. There are no better men than Greg Feek and Mike Ross to find a solution. But everything had gone Northampton's way by then. I recall kicking a spiral from my 22 in the first five minutes, which may have been the best punt of my career. One moment it's nose-diving wonderfully into the right corner, the next it takes a violent bounce left and runs dead. Northampton scored from the scrum.

People may also overlook Reader's overall urgency and how he set the pace. Of course, they will recall Seánie's ball-handling abilities. He was excellent. Jenno had a significant impact off the bench. Jamie was also clever, albeit in subtler ways. Take his sprinting off the ball for our second attempt. Joe always emphasized the necessity of 'staying big past the ball', which is continuing to sprint forward after passing to stay in the game or, in this example, to block players on the inside. Dowson was irritated because he couldn't get to me while I looped around. Another day, the referee might have called us. Not that day.

That score took us within two points. The deal was nearly completed in the 57th minute, when our scrum walked them backwards in the middle of the park, symbolizing how the game had been turned upside down. We're up 23-22 after I smashed the penalty home from 35 meters. With all that much time left, you'd think we should have won by more than 11 points. However, the third quarter most likely sapped our energy. We'd emptied the tank.

Someone said that at halftime, I mentioned Liverpool's Miracle of Istanbul from 2005. I don't recall doing that. I would have mentioned Manchester United's Champions League semi-final against Roy Keane in 1999, or the final versus Bayern Munich at the Camp Nou. Whatever. Surprising turnarounds are uncommon in professional rugby. In a competition, you could acquire important lessons during the post-match review and then get to apply them on the field the following week. The Magic of Cardiff 2011 was the year we worked things out on the fly, made the required changes, and accomplished something heroic. That's what made it special.

Watch our post-match celebrations and you'll see how excited we were: bouncing about and splashing each other with champagne. And the celebrations lasted another 48 hours.

It was predicted that we would still be wet when we arrived in Limerick for the Magners final the following Saturday. I believe we were largely psychologically fatigued after Cardiff.

I rewatched the game during lockdown. Nigel Owens did us no favors, yet we still did not perform well. We desperately wanted to complete a double, but Munster's priorities were arguably more important that day. They were keen to win for their strength and conditioning coach, Paul Darbyshire, who died from motor neurone disease a few weeks later at the age of 41, leaving a wife and four young children. They brought Paul onstage with them after the game, along with the trophy. Sometimes you realize you have to play a role in someone else's story.

When I reflect on 2011, I remember how close we were together. I recall the sponsors' event in the Guinness Storehouse the night after the Magners final, when the entire squad arrived with partners, all dolled up but a little bruised by their loss in Limerick. But sometimes the finest parties are unplanned.

After the formalities were completed and the other guests began to leave, the players congregated in the famous Gravity Bar, which boasted a panoramic view of Dublin. There is a circular bar in the center, so we naturally formed a circle around it and took turns drinking pints of Stout. We sang, laughed, drank. From there, we grabbed taxis to Darce's pub in town, the Exchequer, where the party continued into the night. We ended up at Copper's, where the Heineken Cup made a cameo on the dancefloor.

Kings of Europe. We had some fun.

Chapter 7

It's difficult to envisage Ireland ever having a more manageable route to the World Cup final than we had in 2011. By defeating Australia in Auckland in our second pool game, we earned a spot in the 'European' side of the knockout stages, with Wales in the quarterfinals and France in the semifinals.

Unlike 2007, when the lads told me they spent their tournament in an industrial area near Bordeaux, we were able to visit New Zealand in all its glory. We also got to see it at a good time of year, in September and October, whereas we usually tour there in the dead of winter, in June and July. Days were longer and temperatures were slightly milder.

The greeting from the locals was very warm, especially after we defeated the Australians on the tournament's second weekend. With thousands of Irish supporters following us around in their campervans, we had plenty of support.

Enda McNulty had persuaded me that I needed to incorporate some fun into my schedule, to enjoy the World Cup journey rather than obsess over performance. When things didn't go as planned in New Zealand, I began to question my preparation.

I wasn't really convinced by the Ireland setup. Brian used to encourage me to act with the same authority as I used with Leinster, to drive things and impose myself. But it wasn't as simple as it sounded. How could I be authoritative in training on a Monday if I didn't know if I'd be selected on Tuesday?

Given how I concluded the previous season, I should have trusted myself more. But Deccie messed with my head by selecting me to start the first World Cup warm-up against Scotland in Edinburgh as part of what appeared to be a predominantly second-string team.

Ronan had a niggle that week, which is why I was starting.

But then O'Gara was called up to the first-choice team in Bordeaux the following week, so I started overthinking everything.

Was this a negative sign? It wasn't, but it didn't take long for me to reconsider my belief in the Ireland setup at the time. I was bordering on paranoid.

Sure enough, I was chosen at 10 for New Plymouth. We won, but it did not go well. It was a horrible night with wind and rain, and the Eagles were difficult, as one would expect given Eddie O'Sullivan's coaching style. The final score was Ireland 22, USA 10. My place-kicking had not helped. Even in severe conditions, two of the six did not look well. The remainder of my game was OK, but those statistics followed me about like a terrible odor. When I was replaced toward the end, I took my seat on the bench, stared at the floor, and mumbled to the person beside me: "Well, there goes my fucking World Cup."

I was carried away by the dressing-room bliss, but by the time we boarded the bus back to our hotel, I knew I'd be awake all night obsessing over missed kicks. It doesn't matter how well you've played in the other elements of your game - and I was pleased with how I'd done. I had missed three of five shots, and in my view, that was all that mattered.

That, and the fact that I'd let O'Gara take over the plot again. He'd come off the bench in the third quarter, nudging me into the center, taking over place kicking, and guiding us to victory.

I reflected on the two shots I missed before the interval, how I had been tentative rather than nailing the kicks. The conditions were difficult, but I needed to acquire these images. I remembered the half-time locker room talk between Deccie and Mark Tainton, which they had no idea I was listening to because I had my head buried in a towel. Deccie inquired whether he needed to change place-kickers. Taints claimed I should be allowed one more.

So no pressure!

That opportunity arose within five minutes of resuming. I committed, and the ball went between the posts, giving us a 9-6 lead. I felt great. The strain on me for that kick was immense. I knew if I missed, I'd be gone. Now I was back on track.

O'Gara came on soon after, but as an injury replacement for Darce, so I moved to 12. In the fifty-second minute, the Australian scrum collapsed, giving me another opportunity from 35 meters out, 10 metres in from touch, to the left of the posts. Again, I drilled it, but it bounced off the left upright. To this day, I have no idea how that kick missed. I nailed the line I wanted. But it moved a little with the breeze. And that was all. O'Gara took over placekicking. You could not complain.

It was amusing yet accurate. O'Gara started well against Russia. Between games, I practiced my place kicking extensively. I called Richie Murphy and Dave Alred for feedback. Richie emailed me a video with some pointers. Dave suggested several techniques to help me gain momentum during the strike. He suggested I stay on my toes because I was having trouble getting my weight through the ball. But all along, I wondered if my chance had passed.

The low moment was in Dunedin, days before we played Italy.

The team hadn't been announced yet, but I believed I'd be on the bench. That's when my frustrations bubbled. Leo took the worst of it.

I was in the bibs when everything flared up, and he was on the first team. He grabbed me during a ruck, and I smacked his arm aggressively. It occurred again, and I swung again. He slapped my face, and the red mist dropped. I grabbed him by the collar and swung like crazy. People attempted to drag me back, but I lost the rag completely. I cut him open just above the eye.

This may seem amusing now, but no one laughed at the time. Normally, after a training-ground scrap, you have a kiss-and-make-up session in front of everyone the next day, and the slagging is constant. There was none of that. It was never discussed. No, not in front of me. It was horrible. I apologized to Leo, and he seemed fine with it. I still felt bad.

As expected, Deccie called me aside and informed me that he did not have a starter for me. They were going for Ronan on this one. I simply needed to continue doing what I was doing.

We defeated Italy 36-6 at Forsyth Barr Stadium, with O'Gara kicking six from six. I received 13 minutes off the bench. At least my place-kicking practice paid off, as I made two excellent kicks, one from the touchline. I gave a quick fist pump after that one. I believed they were significant kicks.

We were chasing the game by the time I came on with twenty minutes left. We almost immediately surrendered an unbelievable soft try to Jonathan Davies. There was a 12-point deficit. We never seemed to want to bridge it.

I look back on the journey with much regret. By the end, I was glad to be heading home. Deccie asked for my comments during departures at Auckland Airport. I wasn't sure if he was seeking advice, but I offered it nonetheless.

Players must be honest with themselves. The World Cup did not go as planned, owing primarily to my actions. I knew my kicking was good enough because I kicked over 90% in the previous year's Heineken Cup, but I did my preparation incorrectly and paid the price. The event made my hide thicker. It also forced me to improve as a placekicker. I returned from the World Cup more determined than ever.

I'd reached a tipping point in my relationship with O'Gara. We were still rivals since I played for Leinster and he played for Munster, so we were almost sure to face off twice a season. But when we returned home from the 2011 World Cup, he was approaching his thirty-fifth birthday. I knew he wasn't going to play in the next World Cup. Barring injury or a lack of form, it made logical for Deccie to select me as his starting 10.

That awareness should have been calming and empowering. But for the next while, I kept hearing the same question: why can't Sexton play for Ireland as he does for Leinster? At the time, I used to ask myself this question. It frustrated me. The England game demonstrated that I was capable, but the consistency I had with Leinster had yet to be achieved.

Deccie was in command of fifteen further Tests following the World Cup, winning only four of them. I felt sad for him because he had little luck. A number of important refereeing decisions appeared to go against us. I'm thinking about how the ref blew us off the park in Paris, or Nigel Owens' terrible scrum call in Christchurch, when we were on the point of causing an upset.

He had no luck with injuries either. Brian and Paulie, his two most essential commanders, missed significant portions of 2012 and 2013. Mike Ross was wounded in Twickenham in 2012, and we paid a high price. Missed most of the 2013 Six Nations. By the time we lost to Italy in Rome in the final, bodies were falling left, right, and center. In the span of a year, Deccie had gone from being a candidate to head the Lions to being out of work. Being a professional coach is an incredibly unpredictable job.

However, as a player, you expect the level of preparation to improve as you progress from provincial to international. Les Kiss and Gert

Smal are excellent coaches. I learned a lot from them and Anthony Foley, who was part of the Ireland setup for a while. However, the job descriptions continued shifting. Les was in charge of defence first, then defense and attack, and finally simply attack. With Leinster, there was no doubt who was in charge.

Joe had more time with us, which was advantageous. But the clarity of his messages and the confidence with which he delivered them were very stunning. Consider how he coached the breakdown.

We became firm believers in Joe's breakdown coaching, to the point where when the Leinster players were in Ireland camp, we were frustrated by the lack of detail in this area. Guys from other provinces would shake their heads when they saw us. What is your problem? Why do you keep talking about this? We are great as we are. However, the grand wasn't good enough.

However, Joe found fault with it. I had stepped to the right a nanosecond too soon, or whatever. He'd argue that a more capable opponent would have guarded it. This is the kind of perfectionism you were dealing with.

Then Brad Thorn joined on a short-term contract for March, April, and May, taking us to the next level. We lacked depth in the second row, so Joe managed to secure consent to recruit a thirty-seven-year-old All Black to take us through the knockout stages of Europe. It was certainly the best deal he did in Leinster. Brad provided us oomph in the scrum and maul, but he also showed us the true meaning of professionalism - the way he cared for his body and the importance he placed on mental preparation. I really hit it off with him.

Brad's most significant contribution as a player came in the Bordeaux semi-final versus Clermont. He was also needed there. In previous years, our pool performance would have guaranteed us a home semi-final, but the venue of the final four games was determined by the luck of the draw. Clermont in France Sunday could not have been tougher. It was a day for fighters, and Brad was one of them.

No disrespect to Ulster, our final opponents, but we knew before the semis that Clermont would be our toughest game. We had seen Ulster's semi-final against Edinburgh on Saturday and witnessed them walk a lap of honour at the Aviva afterwards. They resembled a team that had recently reached the pinnacle of goals.

I had a private conversation with Joe that evening in our hotel. We both knew Clermont was the game. Clermont would have a revenge theme, having lost a quarter-final by a point in Dublin two seasons ago. Nathan Hines gave them insider information. But we had Joe. Games versus Clermont were especially memorable for him. Joe didn't usually display much emotion, but he did during those weeks. This automatically elevated the stakes for me. I was on a mission to outplay Brock James.

My favorite moment that day may have occurred in the changing room at halftime, when we were trailing 6-12. I proposed a play that was not on the sheet for the day but that I knew would work. I can't remember the name, but it had Straussy as the pivot off a middle ruck, passing inside to Rob while running on a disguised line. Joe approved it.

Ninety seconds after the restart, Kearns sliced through and sent Cian over. The sole try of the match, and my conversion put us ahead.

We needed something extraordinary to overcome the Clermont side. Rob's tremendous drop goal gave us a four-point lead, but they threw everything at us. It was an appropriate goal-line siege. Joe even broke rules by leaving the coaches' box to stand behind the dead ball line, yelling directions at us. I had to do a double take at one point while the ball was in play. What is he doing there?!

We still have the videotape. You can see me hopping over an advertisement hoarding and racing out to hug my younger brother. I was thrilled for him, Smythie, Steve Hennessy, and everyone involved. I owe Mary so much.

Many Mary's supporters were at Twickenham weeks later to see Leinster's third Heineken Cup victory. It remains the best-attended European rugby final, with an attendance of slightly under 82,000. They may not have witnessed the most captivating finale, but none of us were complaining. My enduring memory is of the pleasant and unexpected few hours that the players had together in a stadium function room while we waited for poor Dave Kearney to pass his drug test.

Normally, it would have been a rush to Heathrow, where you'd be able to mix with the fans, which is enjoyable but not the same type of buzz. It's good to get the whole staff together once in a while to share a few beers and tunes. Basically, the longer it took Dave to provide a urine sample, the longer we could celebrate our victory! I remember having a few beers and chatting with Brad, who was overjoyed to have won his second major trophy in as many months. We both had our sights set on winning another pot the following week, when we faced the Ospreys in the Pro12 final.

We lost. Again. At the RDS. Again. This one was much harder to stomach, given how it ended. With ten minutes remaining, we led nine points. Right at the end, Shane Williams sneaked past a few tackles (including mine) in the right corner, leaving Dan Biggar with a touchline conversion to seal the victory. He received it.

I was upset with myself for missing that tackle. I overestimated Williams' power and slipped over him while he ducked beneath me.

Despite this, I had one nice memory from that afternoon.

It was in the locker room, perhaps an hour after the last whistle.

I'm usually not in a hurry after a match, unless there's a press conference to attend. I prefer to take my time and complete whatever tasks are necessary at a reasonable pace. If it is suitable, you can seek input from coaches and teammates. It's a good idea to set everything in order because you'll be in your own brain for the majority of the night, especially if you lose. Locker room time is almost like therapy.

The room was virtually empty when Brad stepped down alongside me, poured me a beer, and thanked me for making him feel welcome at Leinster. And then he knocked me over.But it was unqualified praise. Brad told me I was a champion and I had to meet my standards. It was the first time someone had said that to me, and I adored him for it.

It meant everything to me, given what he'd accomplished in the game and with whom he'd played.

I adored Brad Thorn, but I cannot say the same for New Zealand. At the very least, I despise going there when it's summer at home and winter there, and when the rugby season has been going non-stop for twelve months because of the World Cup, and you're exhausted, and you're missing Paulie and a few other first-choice players, and it's the third year in a row that you've been sent down there, and the All Blacks are now world champions, and really, if you don't mind, I'd rather just lay my aching bones on a sunlounger in Portugal.

We actually gave the Australians a run for their money in the second Test in Christchurch. We were certainly worth a draw, if not a win, but a couple key moments went against us. I am thinking of a scrum penalty awarded against us by Nigel Owens in the second half. Mike Ross, who is aware of these matters, remains convinced that the penalty should have been imposed in reverse. I'm thinking about a long-range penalty I attempted with the scores tied at 19-19, seven minutes remaining, and Israel Dagg in the bin. Should we have gone up the line to make our additional man count? And I'm thinking about how fortunate the Kiwis were at the end when Seánie got a fingertip to Dan Carter's drop-goal attempt, which was already wide of the posts. That handed them another attacking scrum, and Carter was not going to miss twice. Sickener.

The wheels came off the next week. Scheduling a few days in Queenstown before the last Test in Hamilton may have sounded like a smart idea at first, but it eventually seemed like the start of our summer vacation. Darce and Jamie were both injured.

Meanwhile, the All Blacks had received criticism for almost losing to us. They took it out on us. New Zealand 60, Ireland 0. I'd never received such a tonking in school, at AIL, or anyplace else. I was devastated. I sat in the dressing room, head in my hands, in tears. Why is this the case with Ireland? I was anxious to succeed in green, but it was one letdown after another.

That's not as simple as it sounds, especially when your lives are as intertwined as ours were and still are. I planned a holiday in Cancún, which is not our typical midsummer destination in Portugal, but I wanted to try something new. I'd also managed to find an engagement ring. Reddser had connected me with a jeweller he knew in London. I stopped by shortly after we returned from New Zealand, claiming Laura I had an appointment at an Adidas store - which wasn't a lie.

She was probably aware of what was going on. If she had looked up the hotel online, she would have discovered it was a legitimate couples' resort. Even at reception, when we arrived, everyone asked if we had just got engaged. No, just the room key please. But she wouldn't have expected me to find a ring, buy it, and transport it. She probably expected me to ask the question with any old piece of garbage and leave it up to her to choose something appropriate once we got home.

The hardest part was keeping the ring hidden for days. I wanted to spend the break together. If I had proposed on our first night, the remainder of the vacation would not have been a holiday. It would have been Laura on the phone, making wedding plans. I was concerned about Mexican security standards, but I was also concerned that if I put it in our hotel room safely, she would look through it. I placed it in a case for my headphones, threw it in the safe, and hoped for the best.

I believe I got away with it in the end. I reserved a table for two at the end of a pier, under the starlight, far away from the other visitors. You could hear the waiter rattling his trolley all the way out to us. It was lovely. It was... romantic.

I have my moments.

Chapter 8

When we landed in France, things didn't seem to settle. Laura's purse was stolen our first day. We were at IKEA, buying some items for our flat, when she understood what had happened. Cards, money, and coupons received as wedding gifts were all gone. We were at an industrial area on the outskirts of Paris, frantically surfing Google to find out how to report a theft to the French police.

This time, I screamed: "Stop following me around, will you!"

I was glad, however. By then Ronan and I had turned a corner. The rivalry was over. We became friends, as did our wives.

Ronan had arrived a few weeks before me and was already familiar with Châtenay-Malabry, our Paris suburb. Jess and the children arrived closer to September. Jess and Laura were pals who watched out for one another. Laura quickly became friends with some of the other wives and girlfriends, particularly Dan Lydiate's fiancée, Nia, who subsequently became our daughter Amy's godmother.

With young children, Jess was presumably grateful for an extra pair of hands. She could also give Laura plenty of maternity advice. We found out Laura was pregnant shortly after we arrived. We were overjoyed.

Some people felt that Jacky Lorenzetti had hired O'Gara particularly to assist me with my settlement, but the situation was more random. I was expected to work with Gonzalo Quesada, the former Argentinian 10 who had been part of the previous coaching staff. However, Quesada evidently felt weakened by the hiring of the two Laurents and left for Stade Français. Racing required a kicking/skills coach on short notice, and Ronan was available.

The time we spent kicking represented only a small portion of his significance to me. Initially, he served as my interpreter, but I was keen to learn French as fast as possible. It was vital if I was to run the show on the field. The non-French players had frequent classes with Ian Borthwick, the media manager who also served as a language tutor. By the end of the season, Ian had declared me the most improved pupil.

He offered a four-year contract extension, which amounted to a new five-year contract because significantly increased terms would take effect immediately. There was a large bonus if we won the Top 14 or the Champions Cup, an increase in rental allowance so we could afford a larger apartment, and a car for Laura. She'd regained her confidence behind the wheel by that point!

So it wasn't as bad as many imagine. I played plenty of rugby and did well. It was also a life experience. Laura and I did a lot of growing up. We had to fend for ourselves. When you're working in a different language, creating a bank account can feel like a significant accomplishment. If the boiler fails, you can't simply call Dad and ask him if he knows anyone who can repair it. You must work it out on your own.

How could you expect everyone to come together suddenly? Some of the 'old Racing' people knew they were going to be let go at the end of the season.

They were already annoyed when Quesada left. All of the newcomers had arrived, including this Irish guy with all of his ideas about how and when we should train, who is always upset if training doesn't go well, who frequently arrives at the club with O'Gara, a member of the coaching staff, and who is constantly deep in conversation with the two Laurents after training.

I created part of this skepticism in myself. With the benefit of hindsight, I wish I had gone out for a few beers with these people at the first opportunity, allowing them to see that I could have a laugh and some banter. However, forging new connections has never been simple for me. It reminded me of the rocky beginning I had at Mary's all those years ago.

We went on a week-long preseason trip that was half training camp and part team bonding. I went to bed early, either because I wanted to appear ultra-professional, or perhaps because I was shy. Looking back, I wish I'd stayed up, drank a few beers, and demonstrated my more sociable qualities.

Nonetheless, I was well aware that I had been employed to perform a certain task. Everyone knew I was on a big salary - Jamie Roberts used to call me 'Johnny Cash' - and my part of the agreement was to set high standards and foster a no-excuses mentality. Jacky stated that I was there mostly as a player, but they also signed me for leadership and to try to change the culture. I figured that if I offered everything I had to the cause, the players would realize I was there for the right reasons. However, there are other approaches to gaining people's support. I know that now. Everyone is a genius in retrospect.

So there was always some difference between me and the 'old Racing' folks. You'd come into a changing room and detect a difference in vibe, indicating that they'd been talking about you. Alternatively, they'd converse in French at a pace that kept you out of the loop.

The French believed losing at home was the worst thing you could do. I'll never forget driving into the club with Dan Lydiate on a Monday morning after we were defeated by Grenoble in Colombes. The training pitch was covered with tackling suits. You play at 9 p.m. on a Saturday night, and by Monday morning, it's one-on-one tackling, just pounding each other, as punishment for being defeated at home. Nuts. But both Laurents had recently won the Top 14 with Castres. They claimed to know what they were doing.

They seemed like decent folks. I had more dealings with Laurent Labit, who was in charge of the backs. Toto Travers was a nice guy, and I enjoyed how he always made Laura feel comfortable at the club. But they were quite hot and frigid. When things were going well, they'd converse with me while I was out kicking after training; when things were poor, they'd ignore you completely. They appeared to swing from one extreme to the other, often in the course of a single day.

To be fair, my interactions with others were overly emotional. I was constantly complaining to Simon Raiwalui about the way we were doing things. Like the crazy setup we had for home games, when we'd spend nearly the whole day together preparing for an evening kickoff. Colombes, a dilapidated old stadium in desperate need of repainting, is a thirty-five-minute drive from the club's training facility, and the Laurents were terrified that if we waited until the afternoon to bus there, we'd be stuck in Paris traffic.

So we'd arrive about 10 a.m., drop our bags in the locker rooms, maybe stroll the pitch, have a meeting, and then spend the rest of the day holed up in a run-down Ibis Hotel next to the stadium. We'd have meetings and eat, but most of the time was spent sitting up in your room, waiting for the hours to pass. I nearly favored away games.

The three of us would sit at the kitchen counter at Le Plessis-Robinson, drinking coffee and chatting. It made me feel at home.

Ronan offered security and companionship. We'd go out to supper with the females or simply go to each other's homes. It was usually theirs on a Friday, seeing as they had the Irish channels that allowed us to watch Munster or Leinster's league games over a cup of tea while the girls chatted away.

It wasn't easy watching Leinster. I'd always wanted to be a one-club man, but suddenly Leinster was my former club. It didn't feel right. I hated not being there for Brian's last game and Leo's last game. I hated watching Mads or Jimmy Gopperth wearing the number 10 jersey.

He said I looked tired. I could see what he was up to – to plant a seed of doubt about being out of the Irish system. He told me I was being rested for his first Test in charge, against Samoa.

That pissed me off no end.

I knew that having him in charge would give us an immediate lift, and that the non-Leinster players would be astounded by Joe's meticulous and rigorous preparation. And I wanted to be the one driving it all. But he refused to budge. He said he was holding me for the games against Australia and New Zealand, and that was all.

There was still a lot to be done to get the lads used to Joe's manner of doing things. There was no more sitting in the team room on a Sunday night. Our plays would already be on flip-charts in the team room: launch plays from set pieces, escape options from restart receptions. You had to know your calls well. Joe would then show us clips of our next opponents, demonstrating how this or that play would work against them.

If you were unsure about one of our maps or forms, you should go question someone who wasn't. In that initial camp, the Leinster lads, including this ex-Leinster lad, served as practically auxiliary coaches.

We emphasized the importance of knowing your details in time for the crucial walk-through.

Unlike the two Laurents, Joe understood that our field sessions needed to be brief but intense and precise. We did not spend lengthy, grueling hours on the training paddock. The walk-through was our rehearsal, so you needed to know your lines.

I could identify players who missed out on Ireland caps because they were not structured and prepared during the early stages of a Test week. If someone missed their cue during the walk-through, we would restart from the beginning. Joe would have us stop and restart up to five or six times. You didn't want to be the man who messed up on the sixth attempt.

I had other issues. I suffered a Grade 1 injury in my right hamstring and was replaced by Mads shortly after halftime. I was in a race to prepare for New Zealand, and by Wednesday, I was losing. But Joe gave me every chance to play. I was unsure until an hour before kickoff, when everything seemed OK. Adrenaline is wonderful.

That was the day Ireland felt the Joe effect for the first time. The Aviva was busiest, despite the Sunday lunchtime kick-off. It was chaos when Rob Kearney touched down in the first half after intercepting a ball and galloping 80 metres.

Looking back, I blame myself for continuing despite injuring my hamstring with a tackle on Julian Savea around the 60-minute mark. I attempted to be a hero, stayed on, and cost us a historic win. It cost Paulie and Brian the opportunity to be on the first Irish squad to defeat New Zealand. They deserved the chance.

I also blame myself for having too many thoughts when prepared to take the kick. After Nigel Owens penalized the New Zealanders for pulling down the maul, I pointed to the posts and placed the ball on the ground near my designated spot - one pace to the right of the 15-meter line, just outside the 22.

These are terrible ideas for a placekicker to have. You should focus solely on your regimen. I ultimately returned to the present, to my main swing idea, whatever it was at the time: stand tall. Hold your head still. Or maybe I was telling myself to commit to the kick and not take it easy because of my hammy.

The wind started up just as I settled in, and the fans became restless because I'd been standing over the kick for what seemed like forever. It was coming in over my left shoulder, as it usually does in that area of the stadium. Okay, aim more towards the left post. Then the wind died down. Do not aim too far left. Another notion. Simply said, there are too many thoughts.

I pushed it one foot to the right of the posts.

That was my final act in the game. Mads replaced me for the final four minutes, and I had to sit and watch everything unravel, culminating in Ryan Crotty's try in the left corner - four minutes that would define us.

I was perplexed. My head? I explained that my hamstring, not my head, was preventing me from playing against Montpellier.

"No, Johnny," he said. 'How's your head after missing the kick?'

Jamie Roberts and Mike Phillips overheard this conversation. They were hysterically giggling at Jacky's directness.

I did not mind. I liked Jacky's passion. You could see how much he wanted Racing to succeed. A few days after we defeated Clermont in the Champions Cup in that first season, I was having lunch at the club with Laura when he presented us with a magnum of his best wine in recognition of my performance the previous weekend.

He appreciated how Laura and I came in for lunch on my day off; he wanted it to be a family club. However, it was not all sunshine and roses. He might lose the rag if things didn't go well. After one defeat, he stormed into the locker room and let us know it. Kicked a table into the air and instructed us all to come in for punishment training the next day. We were also scheduled to get a week off that week. The guys had booked flights for getaways. They had to cancel them.

We got along okay, though. I could see he appreciated me working extra hours at the club on my days off. During my first year, I would join Juan-Martín Hernández on Wednesdays for yoga and kicking practice. Laura would join us for lunch afterward. I didn't know if she was coming to see me or Juan-Martín.

I looked up to Juan-Martín. He was only three years older than me, yet I recall watching him at the 2007 World Cup, where he was the tournament's star. I felt we were on the same page. We wanted to play the same rugby style. I like playing and training with him. He played at 12 in that victory over Clermont, and we worked on some old Brumbies plays with Jamie running hard lines off us at 13. This was the style of rugby I had envisioned when I originally pondered joining Racing.

That's when he began walking towards me. He was a forward, a large man. I was thinking, "Here we go; I'm gonna get my head kicked in here."

Instead of waiting to see what would happen, I threw a few punches right away. We split up relatively fast, but as we were being pushed apart, he broke free and smashed me in the side of the ear. It was a totally cheap shot.

Travers summoned us all and sent us home, which was a poor idea because it meant the two of us leaving at the same moment, both mouthing off at each other. It continued in the locker room. This was something that happened regularly at Leinster under Michael Cheika, but it was a big deal at Racing. The next morning, I was called into the coaches' office to explain myself.

Racing could see how much I wanted to succeed, and Jacky imagined I could have the same impact as Jonny Wilkinson at Toulon. However, there was one glaring difference. Wilkinson's England career nearly ended when he relocated to France. I was a part of two Six Nations championships while at Racing, and I was still important to Joe's ambitions for the 2015 World Cup.

The conflict between club and nation built rapidly, and it was entirely my responsibility. Stupidly, I had only received verbal confirmation from Racing that I would be spared from club duty during international windows. The Welsh players had it written into their contracts that if they were not selected for a Six Nations game, they would remain in camp with Warren Gatland.

When I conveyed the verbal arrangement to the two Laurents, they simply shrugged. This was new to them. They expected me to play top 14 during Ireland's Six Nations off periods. Madness. But they were my bosses, so I had to do what they said.

In previous years, I could have missed the Italy game in Round 4, but the Six Nations had evolved into a four-horse competition between England, France, and Wales. We'd all lost one match, and bonus points hadn't yet been established, so the title would most likely be decided on points differential. In Brian's final home outing for Ireland, we scored 46 points against Italy at the Aviva. It was quite the send-off.

The following week, he played his last Test match in Paris. I recall Joe using it to energize us, one of the few times he added some emotion to the build-up. A minor storyline was that I'd be up against four of my Racing teammates. I received texts from Dimitri Szarzewski and Wenceslas Lauret: Attention, Johnny. Be mindful of your ribs.

The title was on the line. We were lucky to be scheduled for the final game of the championship. By the time we took off, we were ahead on points differential and knew that a win by any scoreline would suffice. And we deserved to win. We attacked cleverly, scored three tries, and then defended like dogs at the end, exorcising some of the demons from our defeat to New Zealand.

It should have been a better day for me than it turned out. I scored two of our tries and hit that crucial kick from the same place as the one against New Zealand, putting us 9 points up in the third quarter. In my fifth season with Ireland, we finally won something.

However, the hefty knock I suffered in the final quarter while attempting to tackle Mathieu Bastareaud took away some of the shine. I was chastised for going high on him as he charged at me, but I would have been crushed if I had attempted to stop someone as large, powerful, and quick as him with a typical tackle.

My strategy was always to try to wrap the ball carrier up, off-balance him, and prevent an offload. In principle, everything was OK, until Bastareaud's forearm caught my jaw. Bang.

I witnessed the crash in slow motion, and it's not pleasant. However, I was not knocked out, as previously stated. I didn't want to be stretchered off because I knew it would make things appear worse than they were, and I didn't want my family or Laura to feel scared. Dimitri had just been substituted, and he walked accompanied me down the tunnel to the medical room at the Stade de France to make sure I was okay. That was very kind of you.

By the final whistle, I was back on the touchline, where Fergus, Trimby, and Brian were hugging, jumping, and screaming together. I just felt a little disconnected from the jubilation. I took it easy that night.

Following a head knock, alcohol should be avoided.

I came back with the squad for the second day of festivities, but I had a 6.30 flight out of Dublin on Monday and arrived on time for work. I was not giving Racing any reasons to complain.

Relationships actually improved in the subsequent weeks. Four consecutive wins, including one away to Stade Français, strengthened our chances of making the playoffs. Winning the Paris derby was usually beneficial for business. I sealed the victory with two late penalties.

We were still painfully inconsistent, however. We traveled to Montpellier in early May, confident that we would finish in the top six, and we lost 44-10. It was very messy. My rage erupted in training the next week when I confronted Juandré Kruger, resulting in a little brawl.

It wasn't as violent as the previous row, but it was covered by l'Équipe, which had a reporter with us for the week. For a few days, my 'dust-up' with Kruger made headlines.

She'd made me look like a dark presence at Racing. She detailed a training session in which I gave Fabrice Estebanez a filthy look after he dropped a pass. She paraphrased Ronan as saying that I had 'un très mauvais caractère' (a very unpleasant temper). Laurent Labit informed her, "I told Johnny that he can give out on Mondays and Tuesdays, but after Thursday, stop! He must provide positive energy and encourage others. But he's tough, Johnny. He is straightforward. If someone makes a mistake, he will tell them.

No one appeared to mind when we triumphed in Toulouse the next weekend, reaching the semi-finals for the first time in professional history. I kicked all 21 points, and l'Équipe was suddenly flooded with laud statements from Racing about how fantastic I had performed. I recall yapping on in French during my post-match interview with Canal Plus, stating that we had turned a corner.

Our season ended the following week with a 16-6 loss in Toulon, but Racing had already begun discussions regarding a contract extension, which was shortly on the table. It was really appealing. Laura had made many friends and was enjoying life in Paris. She was ready to give birth to our first child in France in late June, after consulting a

French gynecologist while pregnant. She had reached an agreement.

I was enjoying some aspects of our lives, but it wasn't working out professionally. Playing for Ireland remained number one, and I dreaded another tug-of-war the following season. I was approaching my twenty-ninth birthday and into my prime years, but I couldn't afford to play an additional forty games per season.

It also occurred to me that I did not like the notion of my son going to watch me play for Racing. I wanted him to have memories of watching his dad play RDS.

I had already received a call from Leinster during the Six Nations. Matt O'Connor, who had taken over for Joe, had called to ask if I wanted to come home early. I stated that I couldn't make the first move on anything like that since it would place me in a bad negotiating position. He promised to contact me again, but I never received a response.

Because Ireland was touring Argentina that June, I had the opportunity to drop the occasional not-so-subtle suggestion in the media. In one radio appearance, I indicated that Racing had given me a new five-year contract, but I hadn't heard anything from the IRFU. That did the trick. Guy Easterby soon called, followed by Mick Dawson.

Mick informed me that the IRFU understood they had not handled my contract effectively the previous year. They were concerned that my presence in France might have a bad effect on Joe's World Cup preparations. They understood they needed to have control over the players' game time and training. He promised me that they would make the greatest deal they could afford. Was I willing to speak? I could not wait.

We scheduled a meeting at a hotel near Charles de Gaulle Airport for me, Mick, and Philip Browne. I couldn't meet them in Dublin because Laura was about to give birth any day, so I appreciated them flying over.

I chose not to involve Fintan on this occasion. His nose was out of joint for a while, but it was almost commendable that I kept him out of the bargain. As a skillful negotiator, he would have pressed his advantage. I wasn't going to be a pushover, but I did want everything to go as smoothly as possible. I wanted to go home and didn't want anything to come in the way.

Philip had a significant card to play. The Union would block Joe from selecting me for Ireland unless I committed to return home the following summer, after my second season with Racing ended. They intended to prevent additional top-level players from heading abroad, and this was one method to accomplish that.

Philip told me that the Union's pay structures prevented them from going close to matching Racing's figure, but his plan was to supplement my salary significantly by building 'top-ups' into the deal.

Where I dug my heels with Philip and Mick was the duration of the contract. They offered two years but I insisted on four. I needed to provide Laura with some assurance of security. I couldn't face another contract negotiation in eighteen months. This was agreeable to Philip. We had a deal.

Joe brought the contract over a couple of weeks later with David Nucifora, who had just been hired as the Union's performance director. They popped in to Racing to meet with the two Laurents as a gesture of goodwill, designed to ease relations that had been strained by the differences in medical opinion over my fitness during the Six Nations. Racing must have been a little suspicious about their presence in Paris, though, given that I hadn't signed their contract extension offer.

I signed the IRFU deal later that day in Marcoussis with Joe and David in attendance, behind the stand while the Ireland women were scoring a famous World Cup win over New Zealand. Then I returned to my seat to watch the rest of the game with my family. Yes, we were now three: Mum, Dad and Luca, who was then six weeks old.

He'd arrived at 6.30 in the morning and I was there to witness it.

I'd never experienced such a weird mix of euphoria and apprehension. You are so unprepared. We hadn't even decided a name. We wanted something French – Louis, François and Luc had been mentioned. But Luc would just become Luke over time, so we went for Luca – Italian rather than French, but at least it was European.

Our parents had to wait a few weeks to see their first grandchild. Ronan and Jess came to the hospital in Paris, and we had a couple of other friends from Racing in to visit over the first couple of days. But we had to wait a fortnight before flying back to Dublin.

It was an emotional return, and the love for Luca from everyone in both families was overwhelming. It confirmed to us that coming home was the right decision. We'd make the most of our second year in Paris, but Dublin was where we belonged.

Chapter 9

Three minutes before the end of our November encounter against Australia, Rob Kearney and I collided as we both attempted to tackle the same opponent. I had to leave with a concussion, and it was frustrating not to be there for the final whistle, since the squad had put in a valiant defensive effort to secure the victory.

My consolation was that I'd had a good month personally, playing well enough to be the only European nominated for the World Player of the Year title (which Brodie Retallick won). Unfortunately, all this was overshadowed by the head injury versus Australia. Just a few months before, in the summer of 2014, the Top 14 resolved to tighten their guidelines for handling brain injuries. The incident that most likely caused the problem occurred during a game I was playing for Racing in the Top 14 quarterfinals versus Toulouse. Florian Fritz, their international centre, had left the field after sustaining a suspected concussion but was later allowed to rejoin. The Top 14's medical committee has now mandated a twelve-week hiatus for anyone who has sustained four concussions in a year. The technique was created to limit the occurrence of concussions by raising awareness of their dangers and ensuring that athletes had enough time to recover from 'les commotions cérébrales'. I never imagined I'd be the effort's poster boy.

In France, Jean-François Chermann, a neurologist led the effort. Dr Chermann, who was watching the Australia play from Paris, noticed the clash of heads and saw me stretch my arm upwards while receiving medical assistance. This was a classic indication of brain damage known as 'tonic posturing'. When I returned to racing that week, the club doctor gave me Dr. Chermann's phone and instructed me to schedule an appointment.

I had a fantastic experience with Dr. Chermann. He was very attentive and texted me daily to check on my health. We met every few weeks and had engaging chats. I'm interested in neurology and how it relates to contact sports, which is one of the reasons I got along well with Chermann during our regular meetings. Since I aspired to be a doctor, I've been fascinated by how the human body works. I suppose Dr. Chermann enjoyed practicing his English on me, and I enjoyed practicing mine French on him. (In 2021, Dr. Chermann made extremely inappropriate and false comments about me having 'approximately thirty concussions' in my career. He later repudiated the comment, but it didn't undo all the damage.

When we met in 2014, I was very open with him. He was already aware of my encounter with Mathieu Bastareaud the previous March. He was aware that I had a cracked jaw after a collision with Toulon's Josua Tuisova in August. I had no concussion symptoms, but Dr. Chermann claimed a collision of heads of that magnitude could not be ignored.

I readily mentioned another head-on collision against Argentina in June, and Eoin Reddan's practice box-kick to the side of my head while we were warming up for the Australia game. I had been kneeling on the touchline, putting a ball on the kicking tee, when Redder fired it. Whack.

The accident with Redder had no concussion symptoms. However, it gave me a migraine 'aura'. I've kept this out of the public domain until now: I suffer from migraines. It's in the family. My grandmother Brenda in Listowel suffered from it. Mark, my brother, used to experience blurred vision or headaches after eating cheese or chocolate.

A head impact can also produce a migraine. On a few instances while playing rugby, I had a rather mild hit that created an aura. I would feel OK at first, but my eyesight would gradually become distorted, similar to what happens when you gaze at a bright light and then turn away. It might linger a few minutes and make certain rugby moves difficult.

I've taken penalties when I couldn't focus on the ball's sweet spot. In these instances, you rely solely on your wits, waiting for your vision to return to normal, which it always does. You're only surviving moment to moment, frightened that if you cry for help, your game would be over. And how would you feel if your vision returns to 20/20 as you walk off the field and there is nothing wrong with you anymore?

These migraine auras were occasionally followed by a migraine headache, but they lacked any of the symptoms associated with concussion, such as memory loss, confusion, dizziness, or nausea. Anyone observing would miss the blow to the head. I might perform a typical tackle and suddenly, out of nowhere, the aura appears. I'm not the only one I know whose game affected it. (I won't name the others I know about because their medical information is private.)

As an example, I told Dr. Chermann about the episode with Eoin Reddan, which involved a brief migraine aura. I quickly regretted being so honest. Dr. Chermann added it to the list, which currently has five items for 2014. I argued that it should have been three, but he was unwilling to turn. In accordance with France's new policy, he informed me that I would be out of action for twelve weeks.

I immediately began counting back the weeks from our Six Nations opener in Rome on February 7th, and realized I would not make it. The best I could hope for was to return to action in Dublin the next week. Against France. Who else? I called Joe to share the bad news.

Everyone in rugby knows a lot more about concussions now than they did when I first started playing. I didn't have to look far to notice the symptoms of several brain injuries. A couple of my Leinster teammates were forced to retire early due to concussions.

There is no doubt that advances in American football increased rugby players' knowledge of concussions. In 2013, the NFL resolved a $765 million class action lawsuit brought by former players suffering from dementia, depression, CTE, and other horrible maladies due to frequent head contact while playing football. We all watched Will Smith's movie Concussion. We read the articles. Actually, I did.

What I can tell for certain is that I never deliberately placed myself in danger by playing too soon after a concussion; my health was never jeopardized by any medic or coach; and I have never experienced any delayed symptoms since returning to play post-concussion.

One result of increased concussion awareness was a significant reduction in physical contact in training, with almost no body-on-body collisions during field sessions with Leinster and Ireland. There was also an increasingly sophisticated system for recognizing probable brain injuries and taking proper action, though admittedly, much of this sector of science remains educated guessing.

Dr. Chermann performed numerous tests on me, some of which were physical in nature and others of which were for cognitive function, such as my ability to recall numerical or word sequences. Every professional rugby player will undergo 'baseline' testing at the start of the season, the results of which can be used as a reference point if the player sustains a suspected concussion. Back then, there were stories about guys purposefully submitting mediocre baseline results to increase their chances of 'beating' concussion tests and not missing any games. My opponent could never accomplish this. Typically, I took delight in getting the highest 'cog-test' results, whether at Leinster or Racing.

One of the primary reasons I became council president of the International Rugby Players, the players' representation group, was to guarantee that player welfare stays at the forefront of the sport's interests. Naturally, I'm interested in what science and doctors are attempting to limit the incidence of concussions and enhance diagnosis, such as the 'instrumented' gumshields worn in the 2024 Six Nations, which include integrated impact sensors and radio transmitters.

Later in 2014, at IRFU's request, I met with two independent neurologists in Dublin: Professor Tim Lynch and Professor Dan Healy. I've since spoken with another UK expert, Professor Tony Belli, who has been at the forefront of research into concussions in sports. His consultation was quite reassuring.

At first, there was pity for me at Racing. They'd witnessed the clash of heads against Australia. They understood that being out of action was not my choice. They noticed that when I was cleared for non-contact training, I came to the gym every day of the week and worked hard.

Then there was slagging. Jamie Roberts gave me the name Johnny Vacances, which was unusual because I had previously called him Jamie Vacances due to his laid-back personality. Now he was turning on me. At least it was out in the open, so we could have a laugh.

But I also detected skepticism and anger. It comes with the territory when you're the club's highest-paid foreign player. At Leinster, I always kept a close eye on new imports to see whether they had any attitude issues. I used to say that during the first week, I could tell if the new guy had what it took.

Naturally, I felt like I was being judged, too. They saw me at the gym, but also in the team room, drinking coffee and laughing. I had already missed most of August and September after breaking my jaw against Toulon. I'd already signed with Leinster the following season. I would understand if the 'old Racing' people assumed I had already checked out.

I must confess that my extended vacation had some advantages. Laura and I got to spend Christmas in Dublin and show off Luca, who is now six months old, to everyone. However, the buildup to the game against France was the most intense of my entire career.

When it became apparent that Joe planned to pick me up as soon as possible, he was chastised. Laurent Bénézech, a French prop-turned-journalist with no medical background, called my selection 'a mistake'. He predicted Mathieu Bastareaud would seek me at the first opportunity. What a sharp insight!

When an Irish newspaper published Bénézech's quotes, the IRFU issued a statement stating that I had been symptom-free for two months and had been cleared to play by independent neurologists in France and Ireland, the French Federation's concussion review committee, and the Ireland and Racing medical teams.

Bernard le Roux, my Racing teammate and friend, probably thought he was being humorous when he informed a journalist that I'd 'need to wear a helmet' on Saturday, but it didn't help matters. That week, I avoided the newspaper and spent as little time on my phone as possible.

Joe was unable to dodge the reporters, however. He had to attend media conferences and face questions that suggested he was playing fast and loose with my health. I know Joe was stressed since he called me the night before the game.

'Look, are you okay to play tomorrow, Johnny?' he asked. 'I'm getting it in the ear from playing you. Some argue that throwing you into such a high-risk game is unfair to you and your family.

I told him that was all BS and that I was ready to depart.

Bastareaud and I were naturally drawn to each other. Eight minutes in, the French rushed to get the lineout ball to him, and I closed the distance as swiftly as I could. Smash. But I stood firm, and with the support of Seánie, Robbie Henshaw, and Tommy Bowe, we executed the choking tackle and gained the decision from the ref. Scrum Ireland. The crowd went berserk, and I got into the game. All doubts and nerves are gone. Significant alleviation.

However, that did not mark the end of my relationship with Bastareaud. We were 12-6 up early in the second half and on the attack when Conor Murray fed me as I ran towards the former Wanderers corner. Rob was free to go outside, but I slipped back inside and banged heads with Bastareaud. It was probably a red card for him in today's money - he was upright - and I came out worse, with blood streaming from a cut above my eye.

I left for an HIA and returned ten minutes later, completely stitched and patched up. When I returned to the side of the pitch, preparing to replace Mads, I heard a shout from the fans. And I recall delivering a fist pump after converting a penalty from wide on the right to make it 18-6 in the fourth quarter. That was one of the most rewarding kicks in my career. Receiving the man-of-the-match award was the cherry on top.

The next morning was the most sore I'd ever felt after a game; ice baths and rub-downs can only provide so much relief after going straight into a Six Nations game after a twelve-week hiatus. I nevertheless played the entire 80 minutes for Racing against Clermont the next week, although everyone else was having a bad week. Not that I was complaining. With England the following Sunday, I had eight days to recover for a game that was already being hyped as a Grand Slam decider. And we were only round three.

Mads replaced me after only 55 minutes: I had slightly pulled my hamstring on a conversion that put us 19-3 ahead and cruising. It was our first victory over England in four years and it proved Joe was way ahead of the game. He identified an area where we could outperform them - in the air - and designed a strategy to leverage that advantage.

Joe would eventually face criticism for our reliance on kick-and-chase, particularly box-kicking. I believe he was surprised by that. He believed he was capitalizing on Irish talent and wanted Irish rugby fans to get into it. He observed that we now had two converted full-backs in midfield, Robbie and Jared Payne, and excellent aerial players in Rob, Lukey, Zeebs, and Tommy. We worked hard to improve our punting accuracy, and our chasing time and technique. We were rewarded when Robbie lunged for Conor's chip and scored the game's only try against England.

That placed us on track for our second Six Nations triumph in two attempts under Joe. My only regret is that there was no Slam. Next, we lost in Cardiff, a game notable for the Welsh defence's prowess. I also remember Wayne Barnes, who was officiating our championship game for the second time.

I rated Wayne when I saw him ref in the Premiership. Every ref has off days, and Wayne seemed to have a few of them when Ireland or Leinster were involved. That day, he blew us out of the park for the opening twenty minutes, particularly at the breakdown, leaving us down 12-0. We lost 23–16.

It meant we didn't have control over our destiny on the last Saturday, as Wales and England were even on 6 points. It all came down to points differential, and England had the benefit of playing last, at home against France.

That was a strange old week. From deflation after Cardiff, we moved on to the liberation of Edinburgh, where we knew we needed to not just win, but win decisively. A variety of numbers were bandied around, all of which were hypothetical. Joe chose to address it head on, telling us that we needed to shoot for a 15-point victory. Just before kick-off, the figure had to be revised upward: Wales had defeated Italy by 41 points, so we now required a winning margin of at least 21 to get ahead of Wales. (England would then have to crush France to surpass us.) Joe entered the dressing room two minutes before we left and delivered the terrible news. I remember thinking back then that beating the Scots by 21 or more was almost impossible.

Winning alone at Murrayfield was difficult enough.

We defeated Scotland 40-10, flinging the ball around at every chance, resulting in an overall point differential of +63. It meant England would have to defeat the French in Paris by 26 points or more to finish ahead of us. While most people focused on our attack, we were ultimately saved by Jamie Heaslip's magnificent try-saving tackle on Stuart Hogg in the corner. That one tackle also saved my blushes by drawing attention away from the two penalties I had missed. I experienced a migraine aura for approximately fifteen minutes in the second half, and for the two kicks I took during that time, I half-closed one eye to try to decrease the blurring impact.

We watched the England match in a function room at Murrayfield, or at least some of us did; Pete O'Mahony had his back to the screen for the majority of it. It came to the wire, of course. Yoann Huget scared us by tapping and going close to his own line in the last seconds, but Rory Kockott put us out of our misery by taking the ball off the pitch.

I recall feeling sad for the Scottish lads, who had been forced to sit through another game after being defeated on their home turf, only to watch us leap around and hug each other. We were pleased with ourselves.

Okay, so it wasn't a Slam, and it felt strange returning to the ground to claim the trophy in front of the thousands of Irish fans who had gathered at Murrayfield to watch the final game and discover if we had won the title. But I am sure they were delighted they stayed to see us lift the trophy and celebrate with us for a bit. We were European champions for the second year in a row, and this time it was during the World Cup.

We knew we had the world's best coach. Paulie was the best captain I've ever had; he was tactically astute and an inspirational speaker. When Paulie was on the team, we always performed better. Players hoped to impress him. At least, I did.

Everyone upped their game. I've learned so much from him. We had a good balance of youth and expertise. We were in a fairly decent situation.

Racing was not in the worst of shape, either, since it remained in the Top 14 and in Europe. If we could win a trophy, I'd consider the venture a success. Everything fell apart on a bright Sunday in April at Colombes, when we lost a European Champions Cup quarter-final against Saracens.

Sarries had not reached their prime at the time, and they were missing Owen Farrell. I expected us to win. I could envision a semi in Clermont - difficult but not impossible. The other semifinal resembled Toulon and Leinster. Interesting possibilities? Not for long.

I felt as ill as a dog the morning of the quarterfinal. I told Ronan when he came to pick me up. I was planning to stay at home, but he suggested I come and report to the club doctor. When I explained my symptoms to Dr. Laborderie, he almost looked through me. It was as if he did not hear me. The message was plain. I'd have to be missing a limb before they'd contemplate removing me from the game.

I attempted and failed to eat, slept in one of the hospital rooms, took the team bus to Colombes, nearly vomited up in the dressing room before the game, and then threw up at halftime. In the circumstances, I believed I played well, and we were up 11-9 heading down the straight. The coaches then chose to replace me with three minutes left on the clock, although the task was still incomplete. I would have understood if they had withdrawn me at halftime or fifty minutes because I was suffering. But three minutes from the end after going so long?

At this moment, it's clear that you're playing in your opponents' half, or as close to the touchline as possible. But no, we worked the ball into the middle of the park so that when the penalty was ultimately awarded to Saracens, it was just within Marcelo Bosch's reach. The final score was Racing 11, Saracens 12. Sickener.

There were still months left in the season, but that defeat felt like the start of the end. When the two Laurents spoke to the media after the game, they made no mention of the fact that I had shown up there despite being sick. It felt like I was being blamed for the loss. That really annoyed me.

We still had the Top 14 to contend for, but I could sense the feelings from some of the French players on the squad, and the occasional hint from Ronan. Sexton is returning to Ireland. Do we need him? The coaches assigned me to the bench for a La Rochelle game. I remained professional, sure, but I no longer felt like I belonged. I was no longer a racing man.

The irony is that our social life was thriving at the time. Laura had a close circle of acquaintances and was familiar with Paris. But what about rugby? Racing advanced to the play-offs but were defeated by Stade Français, the eventual winners - a painful point because Jacky's entire objective for the club was to be the kings of Paris.

It wasn't that painful for me. I found it difficult to play at anything less than 100%, but part of me felt distant. There was just one thing that truly mattered that summer. The World Cup.

People talk about 2011 as our great squandered opportunity, but I wasn't chosen to start that quarter-final in Wellington, so it doesn't belong to me as such. Sure, I regret my personal mistakes early in the tournament, but I still hadn't established myself on the squad. By 2015, I felt a sense of ownership, which made our failure - and catastrophe - even more distressing.

Our pre-tournament results were not very impressive, but this did not alarm us too much. We knew we needed to peak at the end of the pool, when we faced France in Cardiff, and the knockouts. Our conditioning was perfectly suited to accomplishing that. I didn't play any golf at Carton House that summer; it was all about fitness. We were quite fit. And I didn't repeat my kicking preparation mistake from 2011. I saw Dave Alred more that summer than I ever had before.

We were also confident. This was the closest we could come to a home World Cup. If everything goes as planned, we'll play three games at Millennium Stadium, which most of us are familiar with. There were no concerns about jet lag, nutrition, or bad motels. We knew our finest team, believed in our coaches, and were accustomed to winning.

We also knew we'd have more travelling supporters than any other club, and a large turnout of first-, second-, and third-generation Irish residing in the United Kingdom. Sure enough, just under 90,000 people attended the game versus Romania at Wembley Stadium, with nearly everyone dressed in green.

Without being overly confident, we could see a pretty reasonable path to the semi-finals. That all depended on winning the pool and avoiding New Zealand in the quarterfinals. And winning the pool required beating Italy (which we did with difficulty) and then defeating France, whom we had beaten two years in a row.

Naturally, a few people mocked me in the French media throughout the build-up. Laurent Labit claimed that I was 'uncontrollable' at Racing. A previous teammate dubbed me 'the Zlatan Ibrahimović of rugby'. It's a shame he didn't have the courage to identify himself.

I could manage it all with no problem. What I couldn't handle was a mammoth tackle from Louis Picamoles, who lined me up and crashed my shoulder into the solar plexus just as I was taking and passing in the 24th minute. I promptly puked up my pre-match dinner on the Millennium field before being brought onshore. My game ended. The speculation was concussion, which would require more long-distance diagnosis by amateur neurologists. In truth, I had wounded my groin early in the game, and Picamoles' tackle worsened the issue.

Mads played and kicked brilliantly in my absence. The entire team was inspired. The 24-9 victory over France was Ireland's largest 'away' victory in history, yet it felt more like a home game. The Irish supporters must have outnumbered the French twenty to one. When Rob scored in the third quarter, the crowd went crazy.

However, victory came with a price. Paulie tore his hamstring shortly before halftime and never returned to the game. Pete O'Mahony was also stretchered off following the game of his life. Add in Seánie, who was later suspended for retaliating after a cheap shot by Pascal Papé, and Jared Payne, who had been hurt in training earlier that week and had established himself as our defensive leader, and we had a significant hole in our first-choice XV for the quarterfinals.

In our haste to assess the severity of my groin ailment, we most likely had it scanned before the entire degree of the tear could be determined. I trained too early that week, worsening the problem, before being ruled out on the eve of the game.

The Pumas are usually dangerous in World Cups, but it's difficult to think how we would have begun so terribly if we had been at full strength. By the end of the first quarter, we were down 3-20 and had lost Tommy Bowe, adding to our list of injuries. It was difficult to watch.

I know some would argue that you can't win a World Cup without depth in every position, but imagine the All Blacks in 2015 without Retallick, Kaino, McCaw, Carter, and Nonu. Sometimes you need a little luck, and we didn't have much of it during that tournament.

Chapter 10

So, just to recap. Ireland was ranked first in the world, and we had the best coach in the sport. Leinster were European champions, and I had recently entered an exclusive club that included famous out-halves such as Jonny Wilkinson, Beauden Barrett, and Dan Carter, whom I consider to be the best of all time. I had a lot to be pleased about.

I also felt valued by my bosses. The previous summer, just after the Australia tour, I met with David Nucifora to discuss my future intentions. We discussed his idea of Faz taking over for Joe, who had decided to step down following the World Cup in Japan. Naturally, I was excited about the concept, especially as David informed me that Faz wanted to keep me involved as well.

This was excellent news. If the IRFU appointed a coach from outside the system, the new man may have desired a post-World Cup clean-out, which included getting rid of the 34-year-old out-half. But Faz and I had an excellent connection. He had made it plain that he wanted me to continue, not only for a transition period. My new IRFU contract would go until the end of the 2020/21 season, which is effectively an eighteen-month extension. That would put me near to my thirty-sixth birthday, but we saw no reason to impose limits. I'd just finished a full season of twenty-two games, and my body felt great.

But could I relax and appreciate this great moment in my career at Christmas 2018? No: even then, I found something to worry about. Although the World Player of the Year award was fantastic, I suspect it came at a cost.

I told Laura as much while we were still in Monaco. She had innocently asked me if I had ever imagined earning the honor. Wait and see, I told her. It will be used as a stick against me. She said I was overthinking things, but I had a sneaking suspicion that the rules had suddenly altered.

I had witnessed how the prize had impacted Beauden. He'd won it two years in a row. You'd think that would make him a national treasure in New Zealand, but not so. It seemed as if people were waiting in line to mock him whenever he displayed the slightest dip in form.

My assumption was correct. It didn't take long until I felt the heat. Originally, it came from Munster. Following Leinster's game in Limerick in late December, I became a target for online hate. I'll admit I was partly at fault.

I hadn't played Thomond in six years and maybe shouldn't have that night. I had been in bed with a sickness over Christmas, and I had terrible tendonitis in my knee. But I was now club captain, and this was an important game. Leo and I decided that I should play. We didn't prepare like it was a big game. The squad Christmas party had taken one day out of our week. It's always difficult to prepare during the Christmas season. Nothing in our preparation went perfectly that week.

Our first mistake was neglecting to use the 'poker-face' method, which had worked well in Thomond Park on prior visits. Joe had brought it in to try to diminish the influence of Munster supporters and specific players. Whatever happened on the field, good or bad, we would remain emotionless, giving the Munster players - and so their supporters - nothing to feed on. We didn't bring our poker faces with us on this occasion, and we suffered the price.

Still, I didn't anticipate things to go so horribly. The game had only just begun when Fineen Wycherley tackled me late and drove me to the ground. I reacted by removing his scrum-cap and generally threw the toys out of the cot. In the midst of the tackle or skirmish, I managed to exacerbate my knee injury. In other circumstances, I might have left for therapy, but you can't start a war and then walk away from it.

Because of my outburst, referee Frank Murphy rescinded the penalty and summoned me back to chastise me. Thomond Park had their pantomime villain two minutes in, and we had lost an early opportunity to take the lead.

Frank is a former Churchill Cup teammate, although we didn't get along well that night. He appeared to pick up on our every violation whereas Munster got away with a lot off the field.

Soon, there was another shemozzle at the touchline. Joey Carbery, for whatever reason, felt compelled to enter and participate. I jerked him out of it, causing him to lose balance.

When I watched the video again, I noticed what many others did: shades of Croke Park 2009 and me yelling at O'Gara. However, I was no longer the youthful upstart. I was expected to set a good example. I texted Joey later to clarify that it was nothing personal. But now that I think about it, I'm probably still ticked off that he waited so long to tell everyone at Leinster that he was going.

The fact that Laura was upset bothered me. She thought Joey's situation looked awful and sent the wrong message. She advised me I needed to be extra cautious now that I was Leinster captain and had received the World Rugby award.

This was reasonable enough, but I was still conflicted. My actions on the pitch demonstrated how much I cared. I was just being myself! What did Munster supporters want? For me to lie down and let Wycherley tickle my stomach?

Part of the rush to judge me stemmed from the fact that we had lost. We were still in it late on, despite missing James Lowe for the majority of the game when he was sent out for a mistimed aerial challenge. What if we had won? Would my actions have been courageous? Excellent leadership, setting the tone?

I care what supporters say, even if I don't know them - but I wouldn't include Tipperary's Mr Keyboard Warrior in his Pyjamas, who named me World Dickhead of the Year and was blocked for his troubles. That is why I made it a point to avoid as much media as possible. I was very interested in what other people believed and said, so being exposed to it had an impact on me. I've been that way since I was a child.

I pondered releasing a statement through Leinster to defend myself, but instead opted to contact a few friends for reassurance. Faz assured me that I had done nothing wrong, that I was simply being myself, and that mentioning anything publicly would only add to the story. Paulie stated essentially the same thing. As a previous captain, he had valuable insights about dealing with referees, including when, how, and what to say. Brian assured me that everything would be fine and that I could disregard the texts.

Nonetheless, the thought of failing myself ate away at me. I wanted everybody to understand I'm basically a good guy. Over Christmas, we watched The Greatest Showman with the kids. As strange as it may sound, I began to empathize with the P. T. Barnum character, the person who enjoys a little fame and popularity but loses sight of what really counts, which is operating his circus.

Had I taken too much pleasure in the attention? Coming up to Christmas, it felt like every second night was an awards ceremony: RTÉ, Irish Independent, and UK Rugby Writers. I knew I had to focus on the task at hand: Six Nations, then World Cup. I had a target on my chest now. We all did. Ireland and Leinster - we were there to be shot down. This Munster flare-up was well-timed. Yes, that was a reminder.

I chatted with Stuart Lancaster about my interactions with Frank Murphy, particularly my body language. He stated my physical behaviour was almost as important as what I said, and that I appeared forceful and combative.

Losing against England purportedly set us on a downhill spiral that led to a crushing World Cup quarter-final defeat in Tokyo. It wasn't that easy, but 2019 didn't leave many joyful memories.

Joe often takes the brunt of the blame, which is unfair and partly because his connections with the media appeared to deteriorate. The players must also accept responsibility for not maintaining the momentum we had created.

I don't know if Joe would acknowledge making some mistakes.

Everything is appraised in retrospect. Everyone's an expert once they know the outcome. Joe is a genius, and he made judgments he felt were best for the squad. Of course, it is natural to think that we should have done this or that. I've looked back and said the same thing. Joe attempted to shake things up a bit, telling us before the Six Nations that everything was now secondary to the World Cup.

Some individuals believed that his early announcement of his leaving following the World Cup was a mistake, as it undermined Joe's authority over us. These people had plainly never worked under Joe Schmidt. However, making the World Cup our entire focus did not work very well. But again, this is in retrospect.

The concept of focusing on the World Cup was similar to how we had set the Slam as our aim the previous season, driving us to think large. I believe Joe was also preparing us for some experimental selections to increase squad depth. For example, Robbie Henshaw played full-back against England when Rob was unavailable.

However, having a longer-term goal may cause you to lose sight of what is right in front of you. This was Joe's mantra: the next game is all that matters. Once we lost to England, it felt as if the wider picture of Japan's preparation had been ignored. Suddenly it was about saving the Six Nations.

The other mistake we made was not evolving our offensive strategy. When you're at the top of the rankings, opponents will pay greater attention to you, so you can't be a stationary target.

This was brought up for debate at a meeting before Christmas, but it was turned down. Joe indicated that the coaching group had agreed to remain with the same attack strategy - well-designed set-piece plays and a quick-rucking pressure game - but only improve by 10%. They believed we still had room to improve what we were already doing.

People have asked me why senior players did not confront Joe about this. We did, a little. The Leinster players appreciated how we practiced under Lancaster and became comfortable playing unstructured rugby. We requested if we might undertake more training on unstructured attacks to better prepare for random events. Joe was often seen as a despot with whom you couldn't communicate. We discussed everything and shared our opinions, but we also trusted Joe to make it right. He had never disappointed us before.

During the New Zealand game, I ran to the short side and asked one of our forwards to pass 'out the back'. However, his pass was poor and did not reach the intended receiver. Is it just a case of poor basics? Yes, but this was the first time that week that this forward had been asked to make that type of pass in that situation, so it wasn't all that surprising. We needed to make it a habit and train so quickly and unstructured that the game felt simple.

Joe's philosophy was always to develop positive habits during the week so that things would flow smoothly on Saturday. We had mastered most of our game, including our starter plays and defending off scrums. However, we were not as prepared as we could have been for the unexpected challenges that rugby can present.

What prepares you for it are the training games we played with Stu at Leinster, where we worked in less regimented circumstances to improve our handling skills and spatial awareness. But was I ready to inform Joe that his sessions were not as good as Stu's? Joe was the best and most successful coach we had ever worked with. And he was the boss.

International coaches aren't blessed with unlimited time, either.

Was it possible to make changes with such short preparation windows? We had one camp in Portugal to prepare for the Six Nations, and a few people were nursing bumps after Challenge Cup games. It felt more like a recovery camp than preparation for war.

And England came for a war. They were aggressive, sharp, on the money. We were sloppy – miscommunications and bad decisions in defence, poor execution in possession. And as players, we had to shoulder much of the blame for this.

It's amazing how one poor performance can plant a seed of doubt.

We scraped a win in Edinburgh and then played terribly in Rome, winning 26–16. When I was replaced two minutes from the end, I vented my frustration by kicking a kitbag at the side of the pitch, for which I later apologized. It was a bad look.

But while I was frustrated, I realize now that some of my teammates were suffering terribly from a lack of confidence. It was only later that I discovered how genuinely unhappy people were in Carton House at that time, how some guys dreaded coming into camp, kept their heads down in team meetings and were on the verge of panic attacks. Athletes are human after all. I was oblivious to it.

I guess I was the last guy they'd share their concerns with, seeing as Joe and I had a strong relationship. I always liked going into camp under Joe. I knew things would be organized and I knew my details. It was like getting ready for an exam and I was comfortable in that environment.

And it wasn't all work. We had a good laugh in Belfast preparing for the France game, doing the Black Cabs tour and going out for a squad meal. We then produced our best performance for Joe's last game at the Aviva, winning with a bonus point to give us an outside shot at winning the championship on the final day.

Cardiff was a disaster, though. My record at the Principality with Ireland is poor, and that horribly wet day was the most miserable of the lot. By opting to keep the stadium roof open, we got what we deserved. And this was the players' fault, incidentally. Joe deferred to the senior players on that call. The problem was there were too many forwards in the leadership group.

I said we should let Wales have what they wanted and keep it closed. We were good enough to beat them with a dry ball. It would be like saying: We can beat you on your terms. The forwards, who reckoned we would win a dogfight, outvoted me. It never even got close to being a dogfight. Wales got an early lead and defended it comfortably in the downpour, winning 25–7 to claim the Slam that Gatland had predicted for them.

I haven't had many more frustrating days on a rugby pitch. My restarts were a nightmare. It was as if all the rain went to make one huge pond in the middle of the pitch, and because Gareth Anscombe scored six penalties and one conversion for Wales, I had plenty of opportunities to drop-kick the ball out of the shallow end. It was like a comedy routine, except I wasn't finding it very funny.

Afterwards, Dad asked me why I hadn't moved along the halfway line, to a drier spot? Basically, because that's against the laws of the game, Dad. He meant well but it wasn't what I wanted to hear. I was narky at everyone, including the referee, Angus Gardner. After one decision against us, I threw the ball angrily in his general direction and was lucky it didn't clip him on the head.

While Anscombe was preparing for the shot at goal, I saw myself on one of the big screens at either end of the stadium, just standing in the rain, pissed off. I remember wondering what the TV commentators were saying about me. I thought: I know one thing. They aren't making excuses for me.

That thought pretty much sums up my mindset for much of 2019: defensive. The mindfulness that had been so beneficial the previous year? The meditation, the breath-work? I was still practising it, but I was back in fight-or-flight mode the majority of the time.

I did try to be kind to myself at the very beginning of the year.

Because my knee had flared up in the Munster game, I knew I wouldn't be playing until the Six Nations, so I decided to give myself a proper break – a couple of weeks off, no visits to the gym, a few meals out with Laura and friends. Some me-time! I deserved it. My rugby would probably benefit. I saw it as a mature decision.

As it turned out, one of those weeks was spent in bed with a bad chest infection. Then, on returning to work, I did a DEXA scan which showed that I had lost four kilos of muscle. Panic. The Six Nations was just three weeks long. I was told not to worry, to take on calories and do weights, and I'd be fine. But the prehistoric side of my brain tells me I need to do more, to punish myself to make sure I am ready.

It felt like I was struggling with my body for the rest of the year.

Some of the injuries I got were purely accidental, like the thumb dislocation and the groin strain that restricted my pre-season to one World Cup warm-up game against Wales. But I had a succession of bangs and tweaks, meaning that I featured in only four games in the six months between the Six Nations and the World Cup.

They included a Champions Cup final and a Pro14 final, which shows that Leinster were maintaining standards – well, almost. We were lucky to have squeezed past Ulster in the Champions quarter-final and were then outmuscled by Saracens in the decider in Newcastle. It's a massive regret – our fifth Champions Cup final and our first defeat. Such an opportunity, too. We had an opportunity to go in two scores up just before the break and didn't take it. Instead Saracens drew level on the stroke of half-time and that was a massive turning point.

Winning the Pro14 final at Celtic Park was our consolation. With the strength of our squad, we saw winning the Pro14 title as a basic necessity. The real bonus was the psychological points we scored over the Scotland contingent in the Glasgow side four months before we were to meet them in the World Cup opener in Yokohama.

It was the World Cup now. I was feeling quietly confident that summer. Finishing third in the Six Nations meant our bubble had burst, but it also meant we'd be flying in slightly under the radar.

Being drawn in the same pool as Scotland, Japan, Samoa and Russia was favourable enough; being on the same side of the draw as New Zealand and South Africa was not. At least we had defeated them both in our last meetings.

The other reason to feel hopeful was Joe. He was determined to finish on a high, with giving Irish rugby a parting gift: a World Cup semi-final, maybe more than that. His research was impeccable, as always. Two years previously he'd taken a squad to Japan (while some of us had been in New Zealand with the Lions), so he knew every hotel we'd stay in, every training base we'd use, and every stadium we'd play in.

On the basis that we were favourites to top our pool, Joe reckoned we'd more than likely get South Africa in the quarter-final and he already had a detailed game-plan to beat them, with various kick-plays to expose their back three and so forth. He was confident Faz could get us in the right mental state to meet the huge physical challenge the Boks always present.

This all came out in the chats that we used to have that summer in Wilde & Green, a café roughly halfway between our houses. It's rare you get a relationship like that between coach and player, separated by twenty years in age but united by our obsession with rugby and winning.

On one level it was like teacher and pupil. As I anticipated, he'd criticized me for my behaviour in Thomond Park the previous Christmas, showing me clips and asking if my body language was appropriate for a captain. It still stung. I'd been hurt when Joe hadn't made me captain following Paulie's retirement. I understood his reason. He didn't want to load too much on my plate. That didn't stop it hurting. We had worked together for so long and being overlooked really hurt. I wanted it so badly, but I never told anyone except Laura.

But while I kept that to myself, he would still hear me out on other stuff. I told him the feeling among the players was that we had too many long team meetings with an overload of information. Joe countered by saying we'd had exactly the same number of meetings as in the Slam year and no one had complained then. Very true.

Perhaps it's different when you're winning and the energy is generally positive.

I kept at him about working on our unstructured attack, about introducing unstructured matches in training that would improve general ball-skills. But he had pre-season already planned. Each week would have a theme. One week would be all about ruck. The next week would be all about defence. Next week on counter-attack, etc. But I remember a few of the younger guys asking me that summer: Are we going to play any rugby, Johnny? They were used to Stuart's sessions where the ball was in play for fifty or sixty minutes.

Nobody was complaining when we hammered Scotland 27–3 in Yokohama. The only negative was that I re-strained my groin kicking and went off after fifty-eight minutes. With a six-day turnaround to the game against Japan in Shizuoka, Joe decided to rest me for that game. I wasn't happy. I knew my body well at this stage. I would be fit for Japan. I trained fully two days before the game and told Joe I was fit to play, but he was adamant.

'I need you ready for South Africa, Johnny,' he said.

He was obsessed about the Springboks. By this point, they had lost to New Zealand, so we were on track to meet them in the quarters, as Joe had predicted.

We knew Japan had some excellent individual players, but as a team they had looked very ordinary against Russia in the tournament opener. We weren't to know that their coach, Jamie Joseph, had put all his resources towards speaking against us. This sounds like being wise after the event, but I had a feeling the night before the game that we weren't mentally right.

Rob Kearney and I had just done some jersey presentations to World Cup debutants when Joe asked for the leadership group to stay behind. He'd been given two hotel options for the week of the quarter-final and wanted to discuss this with us, as we had to make a quick decision. I should have stepped in and handled the hotel issue. The other lads had a game the next day. This was an unnecessary loss of focus. I mentioned to Faz and Besty that I sensed complacency.

I'm not for a minute saying we would have won if I'd played that game. Japan out-ran, out-rucked and out-played us. Some of their offloading was sensational. They were fitter than us, too. I just think that if I'd been on the bench, I could have managed the last twenty. There was one attack in particular when we lost patience, and I was screaming from the stand for us to remain patient and to strangle them. Whatever. We lost. Despite big wins over Russia and Samoa, we finished second in the pool behind Japan. It would be New Zealand in the quarters.

We trained like superstars the day before that game. Joe's plan had been right all along. That was the best we had trained in a year. I remember thinking that we would be more match-sharp than the All Blacks. Their pool game against Italy had been cancelled because of Typhoon Hagibis so they'd had a two-week break since their previous game, a meaningless drubbing of Namibia.

I remember saying in a meeting: It's written for us. We have dipped from the highs of 2018 but now we're gonna turn up at Tokyo Stadium and prove to the world what a good side we are. Except we didn't. New Zealand wiped the floor with us. It finished 46–14: our worst World Cup defeat ever. They played like a team on a mission, like they owed us one. They were nowhere near as good against England in the semis. It was like they were against us.

It might have been a little different if a few moments had gone our way early on. Jacob Stockdale came close to intercepting. Jack Goodhue, their centre, managed to defuse an attack just when it looked like a try was on. It was unfortunate to lose Garry Ringrose after a clash of heads in twenty minutes. But the Kiwis opened clinical attacks. Two early tries for Aaron Smith and we were chasing the game. It's the worst position to be against the All Blacks.

To concede seven tries was embarrassing, but the worst bit was that we just didn't play. Here we were on the biggest stage, in a tournament where teams like New Zealand and Japan were playing brilliant rugby, and we were running into each other or putting the ball on the floor. Our skills let us down.

Naturally we took a beating in the media. Not that we were aware of it at first. We were somewhere in the Roppongi district of Tokyo, blotting out the memory. We were upset to lose, of course, but as is the way with losses we stayed together and had a few drinks. When you are staying in an industrial estate in the middle of Chiba and your tournament is over there isn't much to do apart from finding the bar, and when that closes, head back to various rooms for more drinks.

I felt sorry for him when I saw all the flak he was getting at home.

Everyone was coming out of the woodwork to have a pop. Past players that had so much success under Joe were giving their negative opinion rather than protecting him. How short their memories were.

I called Joe soon after we got back from Japan, just to see how he was getting on. I told him that I'd contributed to the World Cup review that the IRFU was conducting, but that any criticisms I'd made matched the concerns that I'd voiced to him before the tournament. I also wanted to tell him that the criticism of him in the media didn't reflect how the Irish public'd remember him.

When the dust had settled, I called to see him with a bottle of wine and a letter of thanks. No coach has had more influence on me. Even at times during the Faz era, it was as if I saw the game through Joe's eyes out on the pitch. Before each game, I wrote down the same things that Joe taught me. Play in space. Back yourself. If there's no space, pressure the other team. That's the essence of his rugby philosophy. It might sound obvious now, and you might hear similar phrases from other coaches, but Joe was a pioneer. He owes Irish rugby nothing. What we owe him is incalculable.

Chapter 11

Since retiring from rugby, I've often been asked to speak publicly about leadership. I enjoy doing it. I'm lucky to have experienced a wide variety of leadership styles, having worked with some of the best captains and coaches, so I've plenty to draw on.

Then there's my own experience of captaincy, first at Leinster and then with Ireland.

I showed these to Laura and she laughed. 'Tell me something I don't know,' she said.

Joe used to make us do these sorts of questionnaires too. I'm thinking specifically of the one that Joe got us all to look at before Japan, where we were asked to mark each other out of 10 on a range of qualities from 'athletic profile', 'mental skills', 'commitment to role' and so on.

What jumped out at me was that the team-mate who had been assigned to rate me had given me just 4 out of 10 for 'Esprit de corps'. This translates roughly as 'group spirit' – I had to look it up, I admit. I guess he meant that I can be demanding and critical of others if I don't feel they're pulling their weight, maybe that I'm too single-minded. That was an eye-opener.

In my mind everything that I do is for the betterment of the group. Is that not esprit de corps? I could also mention the time that I've given to the welfare of my fellow pros, as a board member for the International Rugby Players over several years and for Rugby Players Ireland, most recently in helping to fight our corner when the IRFU proposed cutting our salaries by 25 per cent during the pandemic. Yes, I was trying to protect my income but I was also working on behalf of my fellow pros.

This feedback helped me to change. After I was appointed skipper at

Leinster, I tried to make sure that we celebrated our successes as a group, often at my house, because I'd seen the value of those nights to teams earlier in my career. I also felt that I'd become more self-aware, especially in my behaviour around younger players, thanks to guidance from Stuart and Leo. Learning from their feedback off the pitch was becoming more important than feedback in training or matches. I was always able to take a slag and give a slag – and slagging is the everyday language of dressing rooms. It helps build team spirit. Or esprit de corps.

Yes, I barked at team-mates in the heat of battle, but when I watched the game back that night I was often mortified by the version of myself that I saw on screen and lost sleep worrying about what those team-mates thought of me. I had hoped Faz saw the positive side of my competitiveness, the energy that it could provide. I desperately wanted him to choose me as his captain.

It was encouraging that he'd wanted to keep me involved post-Japan. But I was thirty-four and this was the start of a new World Cup cycle. I reckoned he might go for James Ryan, or Garry Ringrose, or Peter O'Mahony, who was an experienced skipper four years younger than me, with a better chance of lasting the course until 2023.

Then I did my right knee ligaments quite seriously at Northampton in early December, six weeks after we'd returned from the World Cup. I was suddenly in a race to be ready for the Six Nations. When some newspapers wrote me out of the first two rounds I was quickly on to Fax to tell him that this was rubbish. I was confident I could get fit for the opener against Scotland in Dublin. He reacted positively to this – but mentioned nothing about captaincy. Same when he held a mini-camp around Christmas. No word on the captaincy. I wasn't sure what to think when he texted in early January to see if he could call for a coffee.

The moment he offered me the captaincy was special, not just because the honour was something I'd always quietly craved but because it was him that decided that I should be captain. I always admired him as a player growing up in that famous Wigan team. And I'd loved working with him since the Lions tour in 2013. He has played with some of the greats, so for him to decide that I was the guy to do it meant the world to me. The way that Faz did it was important too. There were no conditions of sale. It was just the two of us having a coffee in my kitchen. He was simple, heartfelt and positive . His words have stayed with me.

I want you to be captain, Johnny. I don't think it should be anyone else. You're the leader of this team.

Faz is a big admirer of Joe, but he recognized the need to put his own stamp on things and that meant changing the way we operated. It helped that we had a new training base in Abbotstown, a state-of-the-art facility on the Sport Ireland Campus. There was a new atmosphere, too. Faz put a smile on people's faces after a disappointing World Cup. To introduce our new attack coach, Mike Catt, he showed us clips from the 1995 World Cup, when Jonah Lomu ran around, over and through Catty on numerous occasions.

John Fogarty did the commentary and it was hilarious. A piss-take, but the perfect ice-breaker.

We looked forward to Faz's presentations. He knew how to use a humorous clip to get our attention but always linked it to a serious point, always improving our understanding of our roles and game awareness. The big difference was that we would no longer be passive learners. This was to be one giant collaboration – and that meant one giant culture shift for anyone who had worked with Joe.

Some of us – myself, Cian Healy and Dev Toner – had been under Joe's spell for ten years. Joe chose a group of senior players and encouraged us to be leaders. However, Joe's voice dominated meetings. I liked this. Only a few people would pipe up and there was always the possibility that they would be shot down if they were talking for the sake of it. This was a strength of the Joe system. No talk for the sake of it, no babble. Only clarity. As an out-half this was the dream. Everyone knew their role. End of.

The atmosphere became more relaxed, certainly. I wondered if it was too relaxed. Faz did away with the evening meetings and walk-throughs that had been staples of our routine with Joe. Once we left our new training base in Abbotstown and went back to Carton House, work was finished for the evening. Another novelty was that team announcements were brought forward to Tuesdays, removing the secrecy that previously added to the stress of match week.

But the biggest culture shift was in how we would play, or at least how we would attack. Under the Farrell philosophy, we would all be decision-makers on the ball. Yes, we would have a structure or a framework, but now everyone would be expected to react according to what they saw in front of them, not just me. Andrew Porter, Tadhg Furlong and the other lads in the front row, they now had to decide: Do I make a short pass left, right, or out the back, or do I step, attack a soft shoulder, offload?

This meant everyone had to improve their skills. From day one, we did ball-work in our warm-up, before training, after gym sessions when we were fatigued, plus extras. As much ball-time as we could get, basically. The new method also required a complete rewiring of everyone's brains. Joe had been all about grooving patterns to the point where players were pre-programmed. Now, they would be asked to make split-second decisions in the intense heat of a Test match. This would be challenging.

It was also exciting. Faz had a picture of where we needed to get to by the 2023 World Cup. He said we were never going to be the most physically dominant team but we could build a game to stress opponents and the basis of that game was decision-making. It was brave and it was a million miles from where we were coming from, so it took us a while to get the hang of it.

Scotland gave us a bit of a fright. It was a proud day for me, scoring all 19 points on my first day as the official skipper, but Stuart Hogg blew a try-scoring opportunity and we only won by 7. We beat Wales more convincingly but Twickenham was a sobering experience for us, even allowing for a few unkind bounces of the ball. My place- kicking was poor too.

The word 'pandemic' brings back strange memories. Minding the girls while Laura was home-schooling with Luca in the mornings, then bringing him down to the local park with a bag of balls, practising place-kicks into a kicking net in the back garden. We tried to beat the sense of Groundhog Day by having virtual poker sessions with a gang of St Mary's pals, chaotic virtual dinner parties (remember them?) with Early, Murr, Pete, Bestie and all the wives/partners. When we were finally allowed back into camp, there was the constant testing, the protocols, the 'social distancing'. What a weird time.

Typically, Faz tried to use all that 'bubble' time to our advantage.

We spent so much time in each other's company that we got to know each other properly as people, to open up and admit fears and insecurities and vulnerabilities. That was a stressful time for many people, but for us it created a bond.

Be yourself, Faz kept telling us. Then he'd take me aside and say: Except you, Johnny. I don't want you to be yourself. I laughed, but he had a serious point. He wanted me to learn the skill of knowing what message each individual team-mate needed at any particular time and also the way in which the message should be delivered, the tone of voice, whether it was in private or in front of the group. I had to be a chameleon.

This was new territory for me and it didn't come naturally. After the England match, we had a training game against the Ireland U20s in Donnybrook when I let fly at John Cooney. It was over a technical detail we'd been hammering home in meetings. When John repeated the mistake during the session, I was furious. He wouldn't take it. 'You can't speak to me like that,' he said. 'You're the captain now.

You're supposed to set an example.'

As far as I was concerned, I was just doing what a captain does.

Set standards. Let players know what's acceptable.

That little flare-up was embarrassing, though. At the end of the session, Faz took me aside and nodded in Cooney's direction. You need to fix that, he said. I later made the phone call and apologized for the way I'd spoken, though it went against every fiber of my being.

It soon seemed a minor matter. Towards the end of my first Six Nations as Ireland captain, my relationship with Faz was looking extremely shaky and I had serious doubts about whether I was going to continue as captain.

At the end of October we went to Paris needing a bonus-point victory to win the Six Nations title. This seemed very doable to me. We'd lost just one of our previous nine Tests against France. They were about to turn a corner, but it hadn't happened yet. Because of Covid, the Stade de France would be empty – another point in our favour.

But we got our prep wrong and I blame myself. Because we travelled the day before the game, I decided to go to the captain's meeting that night to lighten everyone's load. It showed on the pitch. We had system errors and miscommunications and general sloppiness. I learned that you can't expect to win if you ignore your detail, especially on the road. Can't cut corners.

Still, with twelve minutes remaining we were just two scores behind at 28–20. I still believed we could win and was doing everything in my power to convince my team-mates. I was in the fight.

Ross Byrne had taken his tracksuit off, but I assumed Faz was moving me to centre, as he'd done in Twickenham.

At the next break in play, Wayne Barnes tells me I'm off. Ross is replacing me. I look up at the clock to check I have the time right and there are still twelve minutes remaining. Because of the slight time lag on the TV feed, I can see myself shaking my head in disbelief.

Disbelief and anger. And embarrassment. This is a game we can still win and Faz is replacing me? His captain? I respect Ross but he hadn't played a lot of tests up to that point. Getting the captaincy was one of the highlights of my career, because it was given to me by someone I respect so much. And that's why Paris was probably my captain's lowest point.

I didn't say that to the media, though I did admit that I'd been surprised and disappointed. What else did they expect me to say? But the next morning at the airport, Laura called me and said the media had gone to town on my head-shaking. I had undermined Faz – that was the headline. There was no holding back. Three former high-profile captains jumped aboard. Keith Wood, Paulie and Brian all criticized me for showing my displeasure so obviously. I thought they might have supported me, protected me. That's Johnny. He's fiery. He wears his heart on his sleeve. Of course he was disappointed. But no. It was a pile-on.

Stu reassured me. He said he could see why I would feel the way I did. Laura was upset by the kicking that I was getting in the media, especially from former team-mates. Dad and Mark were fully behind

126

me, too, of course. Their loyalty and unwavering support can sometimes mean they wear blinkers.

I knew I had to clear the air. I called Faz on Sunday to apologize for shaking my head but at the same time to tell him how shocked I'd been. I figured he, of all people, would trust me in that situation. He'd chosen me to lead. I explained how I felt embarrassed.

Faz kept it simple. He accepted my apology. He said undermining me was the last thing he had intended. He'd just thought we needed fresh legs and he also wanted to show some faith in Ross. What mattered was we had to move on, he said. We agreed on that much.

I still wondered if our relationship had been broken. Would he now pull rank on me for the autumn Nations Cup matches that had been scheduled to fill the gap in the rugby market? From a selfish point of view, it was probably no harm that I was injured for two games where we struggled – the 18–7 defeat in Twickenham and a scratchy 23–10 win over Georgia. I just couldn't be sure where I stood. Was he ready to cut ties, to move on without me? This was where my mind was taking me.

One thing I would say from this period was that I really battened down the hatches. I learned who was in my corner and who wasn't. During the weeks I was off injured I could really reflect. I concluded that it was my fault he took me off. I'd given him a reason. I wasn't playing well enough. I wasn't leading well enough. People talk about the last few years of my career being rejuvenated by not getting picked for the Lions that year, but really this was the event that sparked it all. I made a deal with myself that I wasn't going to leave any stone unturned in my own prep or the team's prep. I wanted to succeed as a captain. I wanted it more than I ever wanted anything else in my career.

Faz had plenty on his mind around then. Even before we lost the first two games of the 2021 Six Nations, people in the media were beginning to ask if he was the man for the job. The way that we stuck together through that shit-storm was the foundation for the success that came later.

The week after we lost the tournament opener in Cardiff was one of the toughest of my career. With ten minutes remaining, I suffered a concussion caused by an accidental knee to the side of the head from Justin Tipuric. As Dr Ciaran Cosgrave led me from the pitch I sort of reached out to hold Ciaran's arm, a small movement but one that got a lot of air-time over the following days.

We had an eight-day turnaround before we played France in Dublin, which meant I could be available if I hit certain markers on the return-to-play protocols during the week. By midweek, I was hitting those markers – but it wasn't as simple as that. There were external pressures. A French radio station interviewed my old neurologist, Jean-François Chermann, who somehow thought it appropriate to say that he believed that I'd had 'somewhere in the region of thirty concussions' during my career.

I wasn't surprised that the French media might chase a headline like this in the week of a Test match. But I was gobsmacked that Chermann could be so unprofessional. Whatever about his opinions on what constitutes a concussion, what about doctor–patient confidentiality? I rang him and hinted that I might be taking the matter further. He quickly made a public retraction of his comments but the damage had been done. Nobody ever sees the apology or retraction on the back page.

I was torn between playing and pulling out. I passed HIA2 and HIA3 and trained Thursday afternoon. But I had a groin niggle and was constantly second-guessing myself about how I felt mentally. I was stressed about the stories in the media and how they were affecting my family.

I decided that if I still had doubts by Friday, then I would pull out, which is what happened. Faz still made sure to let everyone know what he felt about the media coverage in France. 'It stinks, on so many grounds,' he said. 'I'll leave it at that.'

France won 15–13 – their first win in Dublin in ten years, and they celebrated accordingly. We were zero from two. Even if we won our final three games, the highest we could finish was third, the same as 2020. This wasn't what I'd imagined when I took over the captaincy.

Our response was phenomenal. It's almost amusing to think that Faz's position was under a bit of pressure or that my relationship with him was a little rocky or that journalists were telling me to retire graciously. It's amusing, because we won twenty-seven of our next twenty-nine games.

One of the reasons often given for our upswing in fortunes is that I wasn't selected for the Lions tour to South Africa. Supposedly I benefited from having a summer off. I'd needed a mental break and getting a full pre-season with Leinster did me good. Whatever. I don't buy it.

If I'd toured with the Lions, the IRFU would have made sure I got a proper rest and a full pre-season. I could have delayed my return as long as I needed. The only benefit I got from not touring was that it motivated me to prove Warren Gatland wrong. Does the fact that he admitted he got that selection call wrong make me feel better? No.

We'd never had a very close relationship, but I was convinced he would bring me, based on the fact that we had been successful on previous tours. Gatland has always said that Six Nations form was his main selection guide and I had finished the Six Nations strongly. Our performance in the final game, when we gave England a 32–18 spanking in the Aviva, was a turning point for the team.

I'd set a few personal targets to achieve before the end of my contract: to reach one hundred caps, to captain Ireland to a Grand Slam and Leinster to another double. I also craved a third Lions tour. There's an exclusive club of players who have played in three or more Test series for the Lions and I desperately wanted to be in it.

Competition was tight, I'll admit. I expected that Gats would go with Owen Farrell and Dan Biggar, players who had delivered for him before. Quality players and proven winners. Finn Russell was the darling of the media during that year's Six Nations but he didn't look like a Gatland player to me. I reckoned that if Gats chose three out-halves and if he was true to his ideals, I was in.

It didn't help that I suffered a second concussion two months after Cardiff. This was in Exeter, in a Champions Cup quarter-final. Dave Ewers, their flanker, absolutely emptied me – the heaviest hit that I've ever taken. It was a shoulder to the chest, causing a whiplash so violent that it damaged my inner ear.

Weirdly, I was initially OK to carry on. I felt fine once I was in motion, but then, as I paused before taking a conversion, I felt dizzy. I got the conversion but then alerted the medics, who took me off.

Apparently it's very common for an inner ear problem to affect your balance only when you slow down. Running around was fine, but I couldn't stand still without feeling like falling over.

This was mid-April, three weeks before the European Cup semi-final in La Rochelle and four weeks before Gats announced his Lions squad. The day after Exeter, the only part of the HIA that I was failing was the Tandem Test, where you walk with one foot immediately in front of the other, eyes closed, arms by your side. Once I closed my eyes, I lost my balance.

I flew to the UK to see Tony Belli, a global expert in traumatic brain injury and sports concussions, who conducted a battery of tests, did scans and prescribed exercises to improve my vestibular system.

Once I was able to pass the balance exercise, he was happy to declare me fit for La Rochelle, though he did say another week's recovery would help. On Faz's advice, I contacted the Lions medical staff to let them know that I'd be fit for the final, if Leinster made it.

They didn't, but the rational part of me said that my form would still guide Gats in the last three rounds of the Six Nations and what I'd achieved for the Lions in 2013 and 2017. When I saw the squad, it felt like he'd been guided by someone else. Eight Scots in the squad? Based on what? Fourth in the Six Nations, with a win in Paris on the final day, when France handed them the result by chasing a bonus point when the game was over.

I never heard from Gats. He wasn't obliged to call me, of course. I didn't expect a call. Being picked for the Lions is an honour, a privilege and not something you should ever think you are guaranteed. I still get the occasional urge to call him and find out, off the record, exactly what was said in the selection meeting. You'd probably think I'd be over it by now. It kills me to this day.

His official line was that he didn't think I'd last the rigours of a series against the Springboks. I heard another rumour that the Lions had been told I was too much of an insurance risk, that there was a danger that they would be liable for an expensive payout if I got another head injury while on tour. Whatever. I didn't pay attention to the rumours. I wasn't selected, end of story.

I stayed fit in case I was needed, but didn't play in the Rainbow Cup – another Covid tournament rustled up to fill a gap. Leo wanted to use it more as a development exercise, which was fair enough. I then regretted the decision when I heard Russell had injured his Achilles early in the tour.

Faz was soon in touch to see if I'd heard anything from Gats. A few former Lions team-mates also texted from South Africa to check if I was on my way out. I was in a corporate box at Lord's Cricket Ground, watching England play Pakistan, when I saw the news that Marcus Smith had received the call. Two more beers, please, barman.

People say I was lucky. They say it was the worst Lions tour ever, that the players were imprisoned in their hotel by Covid restrictions, and they lost a boring Test series 2–1 in empty stadia. I supposedly dodged a bullet. I don't buy that, either. I reckon the Books were there for the taking and if the Lions had won the series, that's the only thing people would remember. I would have given anything to be there.

6 November 2021 – Ireland v. Japan, Aviva Stadium

Rituals are comforting, especially on a big game week. And this was a big week for me – my hundredth cap for Ireland, twelve years to the month since my first. For the occasion, there were potential distractions. A ritual keeps everything in place, removes uncertainty.

It always started with my match bag, making sure I had all my bits and bobs in place. I wasn't always good at this sort of thing. I remember the panic before a Test early in my career when I discovered that I didn't have the right gumshield, and having to rush home from the team hotel on the morning of the game. One poor game later and you convince yourself that it was down to this small error.

My bag-packing process started as early as the Sunday before a Test match, when our laundry was returned to our rooms at Carton House. The first thing I always looked for were my shoulder pads. I have kept the same pair since we played South Africa at Croke Park in 2009, right to the end. They originally came as part of an undergarment recommended to me by Dave Alred, with bands inserted to pull your shoulders back so that you could retain good posture while place-kicking. I liked the pads because they made it look like I had a proper pair of shoulders. By the end, I simply had those same pads strapped on to my shoulder before games.

Before one game with Leinster, I asked John Fogarty, the scrum coach, to dispose of the caffeine gum I had been chewing as I didn't want to throw it on the grass. I played brilliantly that day and so we continued the ritual right through to my last game for Ireland. After every warm-up he'd take the piece of gum and put it in his pocket.

Then he'd give me a hug or a high five, or slag me about something or other. Fogs are a legend, an energy-giver. Our interactions put me at ease and probably showed younger players in the squad that I wasn't such an ogre after all.

Faz likes to mark special occasions and the Japan game was special for Tadhg Furlong and Dan Sheehan, too – one making his fiftieth Ireland appearance, the other his first. Getting players' families involved was difficult with Covid – even though crowds were allowed back for our games that November, we were still being kept in a strict bubble. Faz rose to the challenge.

With everyone gathered in the team room, he started off by saying how devastating it was that we couldn't have families in to share the occasion. But we had video messages on the big screen from Mum, Dad, Mark, Gillian and Jerry Jr, and from all the previous centurions. Paulie and Church were on site, so they did the jersey presentation.

Then there was a lovely video from home, with Amy and Sophie wishing me well, and finally Luca, with an angry face on him. 'Good luck on Saturday, Dad,' he said. 'They told me I couldn't be there because I'm not allowed. But I'm like you. I don't take no for an answer ...' That's when he walked into the room, with my hundredth jersey in hand, and the place erupted. There were hugs and there were tears. I was overcome.

It turned out that in the preceding weeks Luca had done every PCR and antigen test necessary to be there, with the assistance of Faz and our managers, Mick Kearney and Ger Carmody, plus our video analyst Vinny Hammond. It was so thoughtful of them.

The performance Saturday matched the build-up. No one outside the group saw a 60–5 victory coming. Japan had most of the side that had beaten us at the World Cup and they'd pushed Australia close two weeks previously. This was our first game in seven months.

It felt like Faz came of age as a head coach that summer, though.

He went to another level. He took control of our phase attack, tightening up our shape and our option-taking and getting us to play at pace. He also picked a lot of Leinster players to start, which gave us real cohesion.

The irony was that Faz's attack shape was so similar to the one that Japan had used against us in Shizuoka, with multiple potential first receivers off Jamison Gibson-Park, all with a variety of options. The key was the speed of the ruck ball, and the guy who gave us that was Paulie.

He'd come into the coaching team for the Six Nations and he was the last piece in the jigsaw. He was seen primarily as a lineout guru, but he made a difference in a lot of areas. He sharpened our breakdown work on both sides of the ball. Essentially he brought back a bit of Joe. Joe always said the ruck is the heartbeat of any team and Paulie transformed that part of our game. He also brought our discipline back to Joe levels, going hard on anyone who allowed the opposition easy access into our third of the pitch. Bringing Paulie in allowed Simon Easterby to move to defence coach, which he was brilliant at. We suddenly had a new voice in two key areas.

Paulie's influence could be seen in our performance against England the previous March, but the Japan game was when everything suddenly clicked. They had no answers to our furious speed and skill. The best moment for me came early in the second half, when Jamison put me away to the short side of the scrum and I scored in what used to be the Wanderers corner of the ground. Every single member of the team mobbed me.

After the game I did a TV interview at the side of the pitch and I couldn't hear the questions because the cheering was so loud. There were only around 30,000 people in the Aviva that day but it seemed like the loudest I've heard it. I'd never felt so much love on a rugby pitch. Not having a crowd the previous two years really made me appreciate it. Some of my best friends in the game, Ferg and Rob, retired in an empty stadium. Church got his hundredth in an empty stadium. So for me to get this reception on my special day made me feel emotional and grateful. I also felt a bit for my mates who weren't so lucky.

Chapter 12

It felt like EPCR and the match officials saw an opportunity to make an example of me. I had the impression that they were deliberately taking their time to build as strong a case as possible, but also to make things uncomfortable for me. The possibility that my World Cup would be disrupted – or even that it might not happen at all – was frying my brain.

According to EPCR, there were three separate incidents: 1) the inflammatory comment 2) my supposedly 'intimidatory' behaviour during the presentation ceremony and 3) my approach to them after the presentations. There had been talk of investigating the half-time tunnel kerfuffle, too, but this was quickly thrown out as none of the match officials had even been aware of any such incident. Leinster were also in the dock for their failure to keep me under control.

Before they issued the misconduct charge on 12 June, EPCR sent a letter to Leinster seeking details from my version of events. We duly obliged, and then received another letter seeking further detail. It felt like they were giving me a chance to hang myself.

Paranoid? Of course I was. The longer the process took, the more time there was for conspiracy theories as to who was actually leading the witch-hunt. I couldn't help but notice how much coverage the case was getting in the South African media, though this was perhaps to be expected, given that Jaco Peyper is South African.

I was fortunate to receive excellent legal representation, from solicitor Derek Hegarty and barrister Michael Cush SC. Obviously I intended to admit to and apologize for my misconduct, but I was confident that whatever suspension I might receive for disrespecting the officials would be reduced given that I had no 'previous'. After eighteen seasons as a pro, my disciplinary record was spotless.

At the eight-hour hearing, conducted by video conference on 13 July by an independent disciplinary panel, I admitted that I'd often 'pushed the line' with officials but had never actually been disrespectful. Out-halves and captains trying to influence umpires are just doing their job.

By the time of the hearing, the Ireland squad had been back training for a month, which was a handy distraction. Training was hard but fun and the mood was upbeat. The slagging I took was relentless. Whatever song was playing in the gym at Abbotstown, Jack Crowley and Craig Casey found a way of slipping 'Jaco' into the lyrics as they sang along. In training matches, Faz or John Fogarty would award outlandish penalties against me, just to wind me up. Cue general laughter. I sucked it up. I had no option.

Maybe the lads believed that I'd only get a slap on the wrist, or that I'd be banned from just one of our three warm-up Tests, against Italy, Samoa and England. Maybe they reckoned that taking the mickey out of me was the best way to keep me sane. It was a release, okay, but only temporary. Once a session was over and I switched my phone back on, I'd see multiple emails, all relating to the case. It was a nightmare.

The EPCR team were able to produce a huge amount of footage of me, from a variety of angles – from Hawkeye and from the various broadcasters who covered the final. Edited cleverly and seen along with the statements of the match officials, they made it sound like I had been cursing them around the pitch with intent to intimidate. I hadn't been.

There were detailed statements from all four match officials, all incriminating against me. Jaco Peyper said he had received no apology from me after the match – despite knowing that I was forbidden from contacting him directly. When asked about the phone call he'd received from me on the Monday after the game, Tony

Spreadbury said he'd taken it as a personal apology, not intended for the officials.

Michael Cush assured Peyper that I had 'apologized unreservedly' for behaviour that had been 'completely unacceptable'. He was also able to show the panel that I had been invisible and inaudible to the officials at the time when I was supposed to have been eyeballing and cursing them.

In fairness to Christophe Ridley, he described my approach after the presentations ('Incident 3') as 'measured and not confrontational'. This was my attempt to apologize. The disciplinary committee still reckoned that Incidents 1 and 2 counted as misconduct, with the latter aggravating the former. I was banned for six games, reduced to three for good behaviour – in other words, our three World Cup warm-up games. Leinster received a suspended fine.

I had to laugh when former players said I had been let go easily. During the hearing my solicitor went through almost all comparable cases and found examples where players and coaches had done far worse than me but received bans of one or two matches. We decided not to appeal. The whole business had taken up too much time already and caused enough stress.

In retrospect, missing the warm-up games wasn't fatal. At the time, once I was fit enough to play in practice games, I was ravenous for any action that I could get. At a training camp in the Algarve in August, we had a training run against the Portuguese, who were surprisingly strong. Roy Keane was a guest at the session with Niall Horan and Pádraig Harrington. 'I was trying to figure out which side were the Grand Slam champions!' Roy joked afterwards.

Roy and I actually had a good chat about the whole EPCR thing. He said that if he'd operated under the same disciplinary standards, he'd have been banned for his entire career. I'd put it behind me by then and was only looking forward to France. Subconsciously, though, I think the experience had made one thing clearer for me: I wouldn't go into coaching after retirement.

My reasoning was simple. As an occupation, coaching is more results-driven than playing. In rugby the result is too often dependent on the 'interpretation' of the officials. Is there a sport where officials are more influential? Is there any sport where the application of the laws is as inconsistent as it is in rugby?

I know that reffing is a bloody tough job, and I acknowledged this at the disciplinary hearing. I'm aware that rugby is a sport of so many moving parts and grey areas. There is an ongoing game of cat-and-mouse between law-makers and those coaches who find loopholes to exploit. The balance can't be right if the world champions are content to spend more time without the ball than with it.

At the time of writing, World Rugby have just introduced another batch of law-trials, to improve the game as a spectacle and cut out some 'dead' time caused, for example, by so many scrum resets. But these trials will only work if refs apply the law consistently in other parts of the game for the entire match.

We need to give the ref the licence to apply the laws rigorously, regardless of how high the penalty count gets. I have heard players say their coaches tell them to live on the edge, because refs won't referee the game strictly for the whole eighty minutes. But if referees apply the laws consistently, teams – and coaches – will soon get the message and the spectacle will benefit. Teams playing positive rugby should benefit. Shouldn't that be the general idea?

I had great plans for a farewell appearance at the Aviva on the occasion of our final warm-up, against England. I imagined how I'd lead the side out with Luca, Amy and Sophie accompanying me.

Instead, because of my ban, I wasn't even allowed near the pitch. As my team-mates enjoyed reminding me, I was a menace to society.

Things happen for a reason, though. The England game was Early's hundredth cap. It was his day. He deserved it to be all about him. He scored our fifth try with an acrobatic dive in the left corner. The stadium gave him a standing ovation and a roar that summed up what he meant to Ireland. Luca was one of Ireland's three mascots, so I had my representative. Besides, I'd already had a special moment at the Aviva, on the day that we had won the Grand Slam. My send-off could be at the World Cup, I thought to myself.

I was just apprehensive about what sort of a reaction I would get from the Ireland supporters who travelled to France in their tens of thousands. I was genuinely nervous before the pool opener in Bordeaux. Part of it was playing my first game in six months and not knowing how my body would handle the collisions and the 37-degree heat. Three weeks before departure, I'd had some tightness in my hammy from overdoing it in training, then a calf niggle.

Apart from that, there was the lingering sense of having let people down after the Champions Cup final. Had I been forgiven?

I found out an hour before kick-off at the impressive Stade de Bordeaux. Straight after the coin toss, I walked up the tunnel and into the heat, the first player on to the manicured playing surface. I did my normal half-lap before settling into my passing and kicking drills with Mike Catt. And all the way around the side of the pitch, all along the dead-ball line and back up the far side, men, women and kids in green were going nuts, roaring encouragement.

For me. What a lift. I tried to cherish it all knowing I didn't have too many more match days ahead of me.

During pre-season, we'd talked about the energy we could take from our travelling support. The younger guys, who were going to their first World Cup, kept asking for details from previous tournaments, like kids begging for bedtime stories. Early, Murr, Pete and myself – and Church, before he was cruelly injured on the eve of departure – were able to give them plenty of material. We told them about the hordes of campervans in Dunedin in 2011, the incredible noise at the Millennium when we beat France in 2015, or the way Irish fans had packed out Wembley for the Romania game the same year, and the huge numbers who travelled to Japan in 2019.

Having this World Cup so close to home was a big advantage but I told the lads that we had to honour our side of the bargain and to keep on winning. It hasn't always been this good, I said. We have to make this count.

The game against Tonga in Nantes also felt like a home game. I had another nice moment scoring the try that broke Ireland's all- time points-scoring record. So much better to do it with a try, where you can celebrate with supporters and team-mates, rather than kicking a penalty and running back with a straight face.

Faz emptied the bench early that night, so I only got forty minutes, to go with sixty-six minutes against Romania: not really enough to prepare you for the Springboks after six months out. Adrenaline is amazing, though. I got an extra little surge of it when I ran out again, an hour before kick-off, to find that the Irish support had doubled or even tripled in size. Yes, I could hear a few boos from the South African supporters, but there was no competing with our fans. They had come to participate, not just to be there. They helped us build momentum that honestly felt unstoppable.

When you win despite certain parts of your game malfunctioning, it's a big boost to your self-belief. For once we didn't enjoy the strong start that had become our trademark, partly because we coughed up a few attacking lineouts – big opportunities missed in what would be the joint lowest-scoring game of the tournament. It was a testament to all the great work Simon had put into our defence over the last couple of years.

You could see how pumped we were by the aggression of our tackling – Rónan Kelleher emptying Damian Willemse at the start, Garry smashing Manie Libbok, Eben Etzebeth getting choke-tackled by James Lowe and a few others. That night, we were on it, physically.

The Springboks weren't exactly shy of contact themselves. In the second quarter, Damian de Allende ran a hard line in my direction on our 22. I went low, leading with the right shoulder. Oof. Following the initial numbness, came a burning sensation down my right arm.

For about thirty seconds, while I received treatment, I feared that my tournament was over. With that numbness, you're unable to tell initially if it's a bad shoulder injury or a stinger. A stinger is unpleasant, but it's the best possible result in this circumstance. I was soon back in the defensive line, watching our scrum lock out under enormous pressure, near our try-line. A big moment.

I was proud of my thirty-eight-year-old body that night. In my seventy-two minutes on the pitch, I made the second-highest number of tackles – eleven – and was on the receiving end plenty of times, often in the act of passing, when you're not always fully braced for impact. It was a proper Test match.

We won 13–8. We had some luck, for sure. South Africa missed four shots at goal and we kicked three from three. They had an attacking lineout with the last play of the game and normally they are very clinical in this area. We held out.

After the final whistle my only mild disappointment was that they played our new anthem – 'Zombie' by the Cranberries – while we were still shaking hands with the Boks. I wanted to relish it properly, while walking the perimeter, applauding the fans and picking out familiar faces. I was incredibly sore but we were facing into a two-week break before the final pool game against Scotland, and four days before we reassembled at our base for the tournament: the city of Tours, three hours south-west of Paris. A few beers were called for.

That two-week break between games came about because of an extended World Cup schedule, designed for reasons of player welfare. Some commentators said it dragged the tournament too long. No one in our camp was complaining.

The beauty of having the competition so close to home was that family members could commute. It helped that Aer Lingus were our official sponsors, and we were also very grateful to Hannah Hanlon and Geraldine Armstrong of the IRFU for making everything run so smoothly for the wives, partners and kids who regularly flew in and out.

My initial plan was to spend a few days in Paris with Laura and Luca and to revisit a few old haunts from the Racing days. But we'd grown to love Tours, a picturesque medieval city in the Loire Valley, so we headed back there for our mini-break along with a few other families.

This was our team room but it was also a family room. That's how Faz wanted it and how we wanted it – a place where partners or kids could wander around freely and feel at home on the weekends when they were over. It was the closest group I've ever been a part of.

By the Thursday after the South Africa game, partners and kids had returned home. We went back to work. I was proud of how I led the team in the build-up to Scotland. It's easy to brush over flaws when you're winning, but you'll get caught out eventually – I'd seen it happen at Leinster. So I was fairly blunt about what needed to be improved. People outside the group had already written us into the quarter-finals as pool winners. We couldn't afford any complacency.

I probably needn't have worried, though. The very fact that the Scotland game was Pete's hundredth cap almost guaranteed that we'd be switched on. We had a four-try bonus wrapped up by half-time and led 36–0 before the Scots scored two late tries. They'd been dominated on the pitch and they were dominated in the stands. We acknowledged our supporters afterwards, but the celebrations were much more muted than they had been after the South Africa game. As far as we were concerned, we'd only just arrived at the business end of the World Cup.

I'm still convinced that we were the best team at the tournament, that our world ranking was accurate. I know I'm biased. And I know that South Africans – and others – will tell me to look in the record books. But it wouldn't be the first time the best side in a sports tournament didn't end up winning it.

People have asked me if we were nervous before the quarter-final, if we felt 'the weight of history on our shoulders', if we did anything differently from previous games. Yes, we were nervous, but no more than before any other game. Revisit the first couple of minutes and it's the All Blacks who look incredibly jittery. I don't believe history has any relevance. This was a different team from previous sides, with its own methods, its own psychology and personality. We didn't do anything different that day.

We just didn't play to our optimum, or even 90 percent. It's virtually impossible to do that throughout a tournament. It's inevitable that at some stage you'll dip a little. We chose a bad day to dip.

At 90% or more, it's simpler to remove variables from the equation, like the bounce of a ball or a referee's bias against your loosehead's technique, even if he's overwhelming his opponent in the scrum. Ninety percent or more is required to defeat a New Zealand team who produced arguably their finest game in two years following a shaky start. They had also received good coaching. All three of their

144

tries began in the video analysis room. Who was the All Blacks' attack coach that day? Joe Schmidt.

Later, I read that Faz should have replaced me before the finish. They told me my legs were gone. True, my legs did go during the final 37-phase onslaught, which lasted only five minutes and fifty seconds and had numerous touches on the ball. But Faz couldn't have replaced me in the midst of the attack. And if you go back to the minutes right before we launched that attack, you'll notice that all of my contributions were positive. New Zealand simply shut the game down extremely cleverly while Codie Taylor was in jail, and we got no breaks.

I was grateful that Faz let me stay out there and give it everything I had. And I was proud that we stayed in the battle and were so close to pulling off one of the greatest comebacks. When our maul resumed with around eight minutes remaining, I assumed we had accomplished our goal. Jordie Barrett sliding his body beneath the ball as Rónan Kelleher surged for the line was a brilliant move. Fair play to him.

At my captain's meeting the night before the game, I addressed it as bluntly as I could: we've passed the point when heroic near misses are acceptable. We needed to fulfill what we had always considered as our destiny. And we did not do that.

I struggled to hold back my tears later, but the healing process began even while I was still on the field in Saint-Denis. The TV cameras were focused on me and Luca when he glanced up and said, "You're still the best, Dad."

One of the benefits of extending my career was that Luca is now old enough to understand what we accomplished in my last few seasons and to have experiences that he will remember. I was extremely proud of him for knowing precisely what to say at that moment. He must acquire his emotional intelligence from his mother!

I located Laura near the front of the stand, sitting with the other spouses and partners. She hugged me and told me how proud she was of me. The following morning, I spoke with Amy and Sophie via FaceTime, and Amy, too, found the appropriate words. 'We're sorry you lost, but we're glad we'll see you tomorrow, Daddy,' she added. My heart melted.

Even Dad understood what to say. He urged me not to worry about the penalty I had missed after sixty minutes. Only four minutes later, we were granted a penalty try, thus his point was that the missed opportunity had no bearing on the result. This was open to debate, but I knew he was merely trying to console me. I knew I had made him and Mum proud.

Other words helped me absorb my disappointment and live with the harsh reality that, unlike prior failures, there was no coming back from this one. Faz spoke pretty nice things about me in the locker room and the media. When I had the opportunity, I reciprocated, and not just out of courtesy.

He is unique; he is the only coach I've met who is a man-manager, thinker, tactician, technician, communicator, motivator, and a great guy all in one. Just as I had done with Joe four years before, I called him when things had calmed down with a gift and a letter of gratitude.

The 'afterlife' was very different. As a professional athlete, every minute of your workday is planned for you. In contrast, my new employers gave me the freedom to create my own work schedule, whether at home or in the office. I also have the freedom to accommodate my new athletic addiction, padel.

I knew it would be difficult when the Six Nations came. Our surprising victory in Marseille elicited an unusual mix of emotions, including pride and jealousy. I was genuinely moved when Paulie mentioned my legacy and how I'd shown younger boys 'how much they had to care about how they prepare'.

I was proud and pleased for Jack Crowley, who had shadowed me on my final lap, pumped me for information, and then stepped ahead in his first full Six Nations. And I made it a point to see a few of the guys for a few beers on Monday night after they won the championship.

It all helped, as did the warmth and sympathy I received from so many rugby fans. As I indicated at the beginning of the book, this inspired my retirement post on Instagram around a fortnight after we returned from the World Cup. I didn't anticipate my statement to generate so much feedback that it almost became news.

I saw it as an opportunity to properly thank those fans and express my appreciation for their kind remarks. It was also my way of thanking everyone else who had supported me over the years, including coaches, teachers, mentors, and teammates from Bective, Mary's (school and club), Leinster, Racing, Ireland, and the Lions. I thanked my family, and I had a particular message for Laura and the kids and their unconditional love. I am so fortunate to have them in my life.

I closed by reflecting on the team, our support workers, and the incredible adventure we'd been on together. 'The pain and despair that we couldn't move forward persists,' I wrote. "They will for a long time, but the overarching feeling is the pride I felt playing with such a committed and talented group of players, the best group I have been lucky enough to be a part of, both on and off the pitch..."

This was how I finished it: 'Four years ago, we sat down as a group and discussed our goals. Our primary aim and goal was to inspire the nation. I believe we achieved it. We lost but won.

Not everyone would let me get away with those final words. Some Irish media writers questioned my claim that we had inspired a nation, and the manner in which I claimed 'winning' after we had lost.

Initially, their words rankled. I wasn't just talking about the World Cup in my comment. I was discussing the team's journey over the past few years. I reflected on what we had accomplished during my tenure as captain - the historic series victory in New Zealand, the Slam, the record-breaking run of victories - and I was filled with pride. I still feel we influenced the entire Irish sporting community, not just rugby fans. That was evident from the scenes in Paris and Ireland during the World Cup.

I understood what the writers were saying. On the eve of the quarter-final, I started something similar: We have progressed beyond the stage of heroic defeats. We needed to win. We did not. Part of me found that unpleasant, much as I did after a cup defeat at school, when Mum tried to console me in the car and I shouted at her.

The only difference this time was that I didn't have a comeback or next match. I was retired and finished. When winning becomes an obsession and you lose, it usually haunts you for weeks, if not months. It fuels your next aim and competition. I didn't have that any longer. I wrote about how I felt, which was totally different from earlier reflections. Of course, it was. I wasn't as fascinated as I had been for the previous twenty years. I needed to find comfort in the past. I found it in the memories of those crowd scenes at the Aviva and Saint-Denis, and the words and letters I got. You make sense of it all by counting your blessings and discovering new distractions. Then you move on.

Printed in Great Britain
by Amazon